Granger In P9-AFZ-944

11/9/80 ft

WITHDRAWN

JUN 2 8 2024

DAVID O. McKAY LIBRARY
BYU-IDAHO

JUN 2 2003

MASTERPIECES
of
MODERN VERSE

COMPILED AND EDITED BY

EDWIN DuBOIS SHURTER

*Formerly Professor of Public Speaking in the
University of Texas*

AND

DWIGHT EVERETT WATKINS

*Associate Professor of Public Speaking in the
University of California*

GRANGER POETRY LIBRARY

GRANGER BOOK CO., INC.
Great Neck, N.Y.

First Published 1926
Reprinted 1978

International Standard Book Number 0-89609-100-7

Library of Congress Catalog Number 78-57862

PRINTED IN THE UNITED STATES OF AMERICA

PREFACE

PEOPLE who are interested in public speaking are constantly looking for new poems that can be used for this purpose. Here you will find a wealth of just such material. Only modern poetry has been included, because most teachers and professors agree with us that contemporary poetry is more suited for class use in schools and colleges than the old, time-worn classics. The modern poets are closer to the hearts of the listeners, both in style and choice of subject matter.

"A poem is not truly a poem," says Professor Corson, "until it is voiced by an accomplished reader who has assimilated it." The selections in this book, therefore, have been carefully chosen for their value in oral delivery, and because they express the tendencies of modern poetic thought with their love of nature, and their humanitarian impulses.

Selections in dialect, or selections requiring considerable skill in impersonation, have purposely been avoided. On the other hand, the poems included vary greatly in content and structure, in order to stimulate the mental and spiritual life of the reader by bringing him in contact with rich and varied experiences, and to provide him with the best examples of ideas, thoughts, and feelings. They will show what new interpretations the modern poets are giving to life, what new beauty they have found, what new art they have realized. This book fairly teems with this new and modern spirit.

Each poem is preceded by a head-note containing a short, biographical sketch of the author and brief suggestions as to the best means of reading the poem forcefully and effectively. Long annotations are considered unnecessary as they usually tend to confuse the person attempting an oral delivery of the selection.

While it was not possible for the compilers to include every masterpiece of contemporary verse, it is hoped that the student will find in this book a wealth of material for public speaking, for class work, and for platform reading. It is also hoped that during the reading of these selections, the student will form a desire to further reading of modern verse that is worthwhile.

TABLE OF CONTENTS

NATURE

Contents

THE CITY AND MODERN LIFE

HOME LIFE AND CHILDHOOD

PATRIOTIC

THE HORROR OF WAR

REFLECTIVE AND INSPIRATIONAL

ESPECIALLY MUSICAL

HEROIC

INDEX OF TITLES

ix

INDEX OF AUTHORS

INDEX OF FIRST LINES

A Ballad of the Road

Constance D'Arcy Mackay

Constance D'Arcy Mackay was born in St. Paul, Minn. She attended Boston University in 1903–1904, and began writing in New York in 1905. She is the author of a number of plays and historical pageants, and contributes plays, dramatic criticism and verse to magazines. She was director of the Department of Pageantry and Drama for the War Camp Community Service from 1918 to 1919.

This is predominantly a lyric poem, and its musical nature should not be neglected in oral rendering, although it should not be delivered in a sing-song manner. A happy balance between an entirely lyric rendering and a strict prose interpretation should be sought. Render the last line somewhat slowly, giving full time to the word "all."

OH, a gypsy longing stirs your heart
When Autumn's sounding the rover's call!
"Oh, leave the city and leave the mart,
Come out, come out where the red leaves fall,
And asters flame by each stone wall!
Have done with cares that fetter and goad,
Heed ye and harken ye one and all,
And know the joys of the winding road!"

A veil of purple lies on the hills,
Your step moves swift to some unknown air—
Forgotten music of boughs and rills—
The oaks are russet, the maples flare,
The sumach's splendor glows here and there,
And your weary heart has slipped its load,

3

Oh, bright the sunlight as on you fare
Tasting the joys of the winding road!

Odors of earth when the wild winds blow,
New views to greet you at each hill's crest,
Color and beauty where'er you go—
These shall add to your journey's zest.
And when the daylight dies in the west
A star-hung roof for your night's abode,
A bed of pine and a dreamless rest—
These are the joys of the winding road.

Oh, ye of the town who do not know
How blithe and free is the rover's code!
Come out, come out where the glad winds blow!
There's joy for all on the winding road!

Reprinted by permission of the author.

The Path that Leads to Nowhere

Corinne Roosevelt Robinson

Corinne Roosevelt Robinson was born in New York City in 1861, and was educated at home. She is interested in literary, civic and philanthropic affairs. She has published three volumes of poetry: "The Call to Brotherhood and Other Poems," "One Woman to Another and Other Poems," and "Service and Sacrifice."

The poem below is slow in movement and its atmosphere is largely that of reverie. It has a certain softness, tinged with admiration and affection. The intervals of pitch are narrow, and a gently swelling force may well be employed. While this selection should not be delivered in a monotone, a good rendering will show features of the monotone, in rather low pitch. Note that the ends of many of the lines should be passed without pausing.

THERE'S a path that leads to Nowhere
In a meadow that I know.

Where an inland island rises
  And the stream is still and slow;
There it wanders under willows
  And beneath the silver green
Of the birches' silent shadows
  Where the early violets lean.

Other pathways lead to Somewhere;
  But the one I love so well
Has no end and no beginning—
  Just the beauty of the dell,
Just the wildflowers and the lilies
  Yellow striped as adder's tongue,
Seem to satisfy my pathway
  As it winds their sweets among.

There I go to meet the Springtime,
  When the meadow is aglow,—
Marigolds amid the marshes,—
  And the stream is still and slow.
There I find my fair oasis,
  And with care-free feet I tread,
For the pathway leads to Nowhere,
  And the blue is overhead!

All the ways that lead to Somewhere
  Echo with the hurrying feet
Of the Struggling and the Striving,
  But the way I find so sweet
Bids me dream and bids me linger,—
  Joy and beauty are its goal!

On the path that leads to Nowhere
I have sometimes found my soul!

Reprinted by permission of the author and Charles Scribner's Sons from *The Poems of Corinne Roosevelt Robinson.* Copyright, 1912, 1916, 1921, by Charles Scribner's Sons.

I Come Singing

Joseph Auslander

Joseph Auslander is an instructor in the Department of English, Harvard University. He writes poetry for *The Atlantic Monthly* and other magazines.

Aim to voice the different emotions that respectively belong to the three seasons described in this exquisite poem. It will require some skill to pass smoothly over the irregular line arrangement and maintain the thought-units.

I COME singing the keen sweet smell of grass
Cut after rain,
And the cool ripple of drops that pass
Over the grain,
And the drenched light drifting across the plain.

I come chanting the wild bloom of the fall,
And the swallows
Rallying in clans to the rapid call
From the hollows,
And the wet west wind swooping down on the
swallows.

I come shrilling the sharp white of December,
The night like quick steel

Swung by a gust in its plunge through the pallid
    ember
Of dusk, and the heel
Of the fierce green dark grinding the stars like steel.

Reprinted by permission of the author and *The New
Republic*.

The Squall

Leonora Speyer

Leonora von Stosch Speyer was born in Washington, D. C. In
addition to writing poetry, she lectures on poetry and music.
Before her marriage to Sir Edgar Speyer, she was a violinist of
note.

This ingenious, accurate, and vivid description challenges the
skill of the reader. The irregular line arrangement, in the first
place, must be smoothly passed over and phrased in thought-
units. Then, too, the whole poem is full of quick changes, re-
quiring great variety in rate and force. It is one of those poems
that may well be tried over and over with varying experiments to
secure the best vocal effects.

It sweeps gray-winged across the obliterated hills,
And the startled lake seems to run before it:
From the woods comes a clamor of leaves,
Tugging at twigs,
Pouring from the branches,
And suddenly the birds are still.

Thunder crumples the sky,
Lightning tears it.
And now the rain.
The rain—thudding—implacable—
The wind, revelling in the confusion of great pines!

And a silver sifting of light,
A coolness:
A sense of summer anger passing,
Of summer gentleness creeping nearer—
Penitent—tearful—
Forgiven!

Reprinted by permission of *Poetry, A Magazine of Verse,* and by permission of, and special arrangement with, E. P. Dutton and Company.

An Angler's Wish

Henry Van Dyke

Henry Van Dyke was born at Germantown, Pennsylvania, in 1852. Until recently he was active as Professor of English at Princeton University. In his lifetime he has attained success in many varied fields, having been successful as an author of poems, essays, and stories, and having been a minister, an educator, and a diplomatist.

This poem is permeated with the breath of spring. It is bright, but there is a sort of lazy relaxation that qualifies the lightness. It is full of longing, too, but never petulant. Resignation and complete satisfaction characterize the last two stanzas, which may be delivered very slowly, the vowels being prolonged and attenuated so as to bring out their full value. Be careful to end slowly.

I

WHEN tulips bloom in Union Square,
And timid breaths of vernal air
    Go wandering down the dusty town,
Like children lost in Vanity Fair;

When every long, unlovely row
Of westward houses stands aglow,
    And leads the eyes toward sunset skies
Beyond the hills where green trees grow,—

Then weary seems the street parade,
And weary books, and weary trade:
  I'm only wishing to go a-fishing;
For this the month of May was made.

2

I guess the pussy willows now
Are creeping out on every bough
  Along the brook; and robins look
For early worms behind the plow.

The thistle birds have changed their dun
For yellow coats, to match the sun;
  And in the same array of flame
The dandelion show's begun.

The flocks of young anemones
Are dancing round the budding trees:
  Who can help wishing to go a-fishing
In days as full of joy as these?

3

I think the meadow lark's clear sound
Leaks upward slowly from the ground,
  While on the wing the bluebirds ring
Their wedding bells to woods around.

The flirting chewink calls his dear
Behind the bush; and very near,

Where water flows, where green grass grows,
Song sparrows gently sing, "Good Cheer."

And, best of all, through twilight's calm
The hermit thrush repeats his psalm.
How much I'm wishing to go a-fishing
In days so sweet with music's balm!

4

'Tis not a proud desire of mine;
I ask for nothing superfine;
No heavy weight, no salmon great,
To break the record—or my line:

Only an idle little stream,
Whose amber waters softly gleam,
Where I may wade, through woodland shade,
And cast the fly, and loaf, and dream:

Only a trout or two, to dart
From foaming pools, and try my art:
No more I'm wishing—old-fashioned fishing,
And just a day on Nature's heart.

Reprinted by permission of the author, and by permission of, and by special arrangement with, Charles Scribner's Sons, the publishers of the author's works.

The Chant of the Colorado

(At the Grand Canyon)

Cale Young Rice

Cale Young Rice was born in Dixon, Ky., December 7th, 1872. He is a poet, dramatist, and short story writer, and was professor of English Literature in Cumberland University in 1896–1897. He has since devoted himself to the writing of poetry, poetic drama, and occasional prose.

The majesty and beauty of the Grand Canyon of the Colorado are well reflected in this poem. Be sure, by due emphasis, to bring out the antithesis implied in the first two lines of each stanza. The poem as a whole should be delivered firmly, with a touch of the heroic. Do not, however, neglect the few lyric lines that appear in each stanza. Deliver the poem slowly enough to bring out all the grandeur, and yet not too slowly to mar the value of the rhyme scheme.

My brother, man, shapes him a plan
  And builds him a house in a day,
But I have toiled through a million years
  For a home to last alway.
I have flooded the sands and washed them down,
  I have cut through gneiss and granite.
No toiler of earth has wrought as I,
  Since God's first breath began it.
High mountain buttes have I chiselled, to shade
  My wanderings to the sea.
With the wind's aid, and the cloud's aid,
Unweary and mighty and unafraid,
  I have bodied eternity.

My brother, man, builds for a span:
  His life is a moment's breath.
But I have hewn for a million years,
  Nor a moment dreamt of death.

By moons and stars I have measured my task—
  And some from the skies have perished:
But ever I cut and flashed and foamed,
  As ever my aim I cherished:
My aim to quarry the heart of earth,
  Till, in rock's red rise,
Its age and birth, through an awful girth
Of strata, should show the wonder-worth
  Of patience to all eyes.

My brother, man, builds as he can,
  And beauty he adds for his joy,
But all the hues of sublimity
  My pinnacled walls employ.
Slow shadows iris them all day long,
  And silvery ceils, soul-stilling,
The moon drops down their precipices,
  Soft with a spectral thrilling.
For all immutable dreams that sway
  With beauty the earth and air,
Are ever at play, by night and day,
My house of eternity to array
  In visions ever fair.

Reprinted by permission of Cale Young Rice and The Century Co., the publishers of Mr. Rice's works, among which are "Sea Poems," "Shadowy Thresholds," "Songs to A. H. R.," "Wraiths and Realities," "Earth and New Earth," and "Trails Sunward."

Sea Fever

John Masefield

John Masefield was born in Shropshire, England, in 1874. He ran away from home at the age of 14 and joined the navy. The influence of his life at sea is marked in many of his writings. He has written a number of dramas and novels as well as a great deal of poetry.

This "call of the running tide" requires the use of the imagination and a sympathetic response to the spirit of the poem. Generally speaking, the semicolon marks the division of distinct thought-units in each stanza. The somewhat abrupt close of each stanza will be helped in the oral expression by pausing before the last word.

I MUST go down to the seas again, to the lonely sea
     and the sky,
And all I ask is a tall ship and a star to steer her by;
And the wheel's kick and the wind's song and the
     white sail's shaking,
And a gray mist on the sea's face, and a gray dawn
     breaking.

I must go down to the seas again, for the call of the
     running tide
Is a wild call and a clear call that may not be denied;
And all I ask is a windy day with the white clouds
     flying,
And the flung spray and the blown spume, and the
     sea-gulls crying.

I must go down to the seas again, to the vagrant
     gypsy life,
To the gull's way and the whale's way where the
     wind's like a whetted knife;

And all I ask is a merry yarn from a laughing
    fellow-rover,
And quiet sleep and a sweet dream when the long
    trick's over.

Reprinted by permission of, and by special arrangement with, The Macmillan Company. Copyrighted by The Macmillan Company.

The Sea Gypsy

Richard Hovey

Richard Hovey was born at Normal, Illinois, May 4, 1864. He was on the stage for a number of years and has written many poems and dramas. He died Feb. 26, 1900.

This exquisite lyric should be delivered with fervor. Reveal the sense clearly, but do not neglect the musical rhythm.

I AM fevered with the sunset,
I am fretful with the bay,
For the wander-thirst is on me
And my soul is in Cathay.

There's a schooner in the offing,
With her topsails shot with fire,
And my heart has gone aboard her
For the Islands of Desire.

I must forth again to-morrow!
With the sunset I must be,
Hull down on the trail of rapture
In the wonder of the sea.

Reprinted by permission of, and by special arrangement with, Small, Maynard Co.

Neptune's Steeds

William Lawrence Chittenden

William Lawrence Chittenden was born at Montclair, N. J., March 23, 1862. He began life as reporter for a New York newspaper, but later went to Texas and engaged in the cattle business in which he has been very successful. He has contributed verse and other matter to various periodicals under the pen-name of "Larry Chittenden." He is the author of "Ranch Verses," 1893, now in the fifteenth edition (Putnams—publishers), "Bermuda Verses," 1909, "Lafferty's Letters," etc. The following verses from his book, "Ranch Verses," evaluated by Dr. Lyman Abbott as the best of the author's poems, were written at his summer home, "Christmas Cove," on the coast of Maine.

. Have you ever watched from the seashore during a storm the white-crested waves—"the wild white steeds of Neptune"—as with tumultuous on-rush and resistless power they approached the shore? This is the picture you must see and depict as you read this poem.

HARK to the wild nor'easter!
That long, long booming roar,
When the Storm King breathes his thunder
Along the shuddering shore.
The shivering air re-echoes
The ocean's weird refrain,
For the wild white steeds of Neptune
　Are coming home again.

No hand nor voice can check them,
These stern steeds of the sea,
They were not born for bondage,
They are forever free.
With arched crests proudly waving,
Too strong for human rein,
The wild white steeds of Neptune
　Are coming home again.

With rolling emerald chariots
They charge the stalwart strand,
They gallop o'er the ledges
And leap along the land;
With deep chests breathing thunder
Across the quivering plain,
The wild white steeds of Neptune
  Are coming home again.

Not with the trill of bugles,
But roar of muffled drums
And shrouded sea-weed banners,
That mighty army comes.
The harbor bars are moaning
A wail of death and pain,
For the wild white steeds of Neptune
  Are coming home again.

Well may the sailor women
Look out to scan the lee,
And long for absent lovers,
Their lovers on the sea.
Well may the harbored seamen
Neglect the sails and seine,
When the wild white steeds of Neptune
  Are coming home again.

How sad their mournful neighing,
That wailing, haunting sound;
It is the song of sorrow,
A dirge for dead men drowned.
Though we must all go seaward,

Though our watchers wait in vain,
The wild white steeds of Neptune
Will homeward come again.

Reprinted by permission of the author.

Salute to the Trees

Henry Van Dyke

For biographical note concerning the author, see "An Angler's Wish," page 8.

This beautiful tribute to the trees will surely bring from every reader a sympathetic response. Full, round, ringing tones are required for effective delivery. The meter is such that you will need to be on your guard against falling into a "sing-song."

MANY a tree is found in the wood
And every tree for its use is good:
Some for the strength of the gnarlèd root,
Some for the sweetness of flower or fruit;
Some for shelter against the storm,
And some to keep the hearth-stone warm;
Some for the roof and some for the beam,
And some for a boat to breast the stream;—
In the wealth of the wood since the world began
The trees have offered their gifts to man.

But the glory of trees is more than their gifts:
'Tis a beautiful wonder of life that lifts,
From a wrinkled seed in an earth-bound clod,
A column, an arch in the temple of God,
A pillar of power, a dome of delight,
A shrine of song, and a joy of sight!
Their roots are the nurses of rivers in birth;

Their leaves are alive with the breath of the earth;
They shelter the dwellings of man; and they bend
O'er his grave with the look of a loving friend.

I have camped in the whispering forest of pines,
I have slept in the shadow of olives and vines;
In the knees of an oak, at the foot of a palm,
I have found good rest and a slumber's balm.
And now, when the morning gilds the boughs
Of the vaulted elm at the door of my house,
I open the window and make salute:
"God bless thy branches and feed thy root!
Thou hast lived before, live after me,
Thou ancient, friendly, faithful tree."

Reprinted by permission of the author and by special arrangement with, Charles Scribner's Sons, the publishers of the author's works.

The Green Inn

Theodosia Garrison Faulks

Theodosia Garrison Faulks was born in Newark, N. J., in 1874, and was educated in private schools. She is the author of a number of poems, and contributes verse and stories to magazines.

Where is the background of this poem, and why could it not be placed in our country at this time? In the delivery, watch especially for the proper placing of emphasis in order to express the thought. A slow rate, with expansion of the principal words, is required for the most effective reading of the last stanza.

I SICKEN of men's company,
  The crowded tavern's din,
Where all day long with oath and song
  Sit they who entrance win,

So come I out from noise and rout
  To rest in God's Green Inn.

Here none may mock an empty purse
  Or ragged coat and poor,
But Silence waits within the gates
  And Peace beside the door;
The weary guest is welcomest,
  The richest pays no score.

The roof is high and arched and blue,
  The floor is spread with pine;
On my four walls the sunlight falls
  In golden flecks and fine;
And swift and fleet on noiseless feet
  The Four Winds bring me wine.

Upon my board they set their store,
  Great drinks mixed cunningly,
Wherein the scent of furze is blent
  With the odor of the sea;
As from a cup I drink it up
  To thrill the veins of me.

It's I will sit in God's Green Inn
  Unvexed by man or ghost,
Yet ever fed and comforted,
  Companioned by my host,
And watched by night by that white light
  High swung from coast to coast.

O you who in the House of Strife
  Quarrel and game and sin,

Come out and see what cheer may be
  For starveling souls and thin
Who come at last from drought and fast
  To sit in God's Green Inn.

Reprinted by permission of the author and *Scribner's Magazine*. Copyright, 1907, by Charles Scribner's Sons.

Rebels

Louis Untermeyer

For biographical note concerning the author, see "The Laughers," Page 88.

This unique fancy, built around a single phenomenon in nature, will appeal especially to residents of the northern sections, where the scene described is frequently observed.

STIFF in midsummer green, the stolid hillsides
  March with their trees, dependable and staunch,
Except where here and there a lawless maple
  Thrusts to the sky one red, rebellious branch.

You see them standing out, these frank insurgents,
  With that defiant and arresting plume;
Scattered, they toss this flame like some wild signal,
  Calling their comrades to a brilliant doom.

What can it mean—this strange, untimely challenge;
  This proclamation of an early death?
Are they so tired of earth they fly the banner
  Of dissolution and a bleeding faith?

Or is it, rather than a brief defiance,
  An anxious welcome to a vivid strife?

A glow, a heart-beat, and a bright acceptance
  Of all the rich exuberance of life.

Rebellious or resigned, they flaunt their color,
  A sudden torch, a burning battle-cry.
"Light up the world," they wave to all the others;
  "Swiftly we live and splendidly we die."

Reprinted by permission of the author and Henry
Holt and Company.

Birches

Robert Frost

Robert Frost was born in San Francisco in 1875, but was
brought up in New England. Most of his poetry deals with life
in the North Atlantic States. He is now professor of English in
the University of Michigan. Among his books are "North of
Boston," "A Boy's Will," and "Mountain Interval," all published
by Henry Holt and Co., New York.

This teasing sort of verse—more than half conversational—is
difficult to render, but pleasing when it is rendered well. Bring
out the picture in the early part of the poem, and the philosophy
toward the end.

WHEN I see birches bend to left and right
Across the lines of straighter darker trees,
I like to think some boy's swinging them.
But swinging doesn't bend them down to stay.
Ice-storms do that. Often you must have seen them
After a rain. They click upon themselves
As the breeze rises, and turn many-colored
As the stir cracks and crazes their enamel.
Soon the sun's warmth makes them shed crystal
    shells
Shattering and avalanching on the snow-crust—

Such heaps of broken glass to sweep away
You'd think the inner dome of heaven had fallen.
They are dragged to the withered bracken by the
    load,
And they seem not to break; though once they are
    bowed
So low for long, they never right themselves:
You may see their trunks arching in the woods
Years afterwards, trailing their leaves on the ground
Like girls on hands and knees that throw their hair
Before them over their heads to dry in the sun.
But I was going to say when Truth broke in
With all her matter-of-fact about the ice-storm
(Now am I free to be poetical?)
I should prefer to have some boy bend them
As he went out and in to fetch the cows—
Some boy too far from town to learn baseball,
Whose only play was what he found himself,
Summer or winter, and could play alone.
One by one he subdued his father's trees
By riding them down over and over again
Until he took the stiffness out of them,
And not one but hung limp, not one was left
For him to conquer. He learned all there was
To learn about not launching out too soon
And so not carrying the tree away
Clear to the ground. He always kept his poise
To the top branches, climbing carefully
With the same pains you use to fill a cup
Up to the brim, and even above the brim.
Then he flung outward, feet first, with a swish,
Kicking his way down through the air to the ground.

So was I once myself a swinger of birches.
And so I dream of going back to be.
It's when I'm weary of considerations,
And life is too much like a pathless wood
Where your face burns and tickles with the cobwebs
Broken across it, and one eye is weeping
From a twig's having lashed across it open.
I'd like to get away from earth awhile
And then come back to it and begin over.
May no fate willfully misunderstand me
And half grant what I wish and snatch me away
Not to return.   Earth's the right place for love:
I don't know where it's likely to go better.
I'd like to go by climbing a birch tree,
And climb black branches up a snow-white trunk
Toward heaven, till the tree could bear no more,
But dipped its top and set me down again.
That would be good both going and coming back.
One could do worse than be a swinger of birches.

Reprinted by permission of Henry Holt and Company.

The Joy of the Hills

Edwin Markham

For biographical note concerning the author, see "The Man with the Hoe," page 103.

There is joy and expansion in this poem. Deliver it with sweep and abandon. Because the scene changes so often, it is best to read this selection from the book.

I RIDE on the mountain-tops, I ride;
I have found my life and am satisfied.

Onward I ride in the blowing oats,
Checking the field-lark's rippling notes—
         Lightly I sweep
         From steep to steep:
Over my head through the branches high
Come glimpses of a rushing sky;
The tall oats brush my horse's flanks;
Wild poppies crowd on the sunny banks;
A bee booms out of the scented grass;
A jay laughs with me as I pass.

I ride on the hills, I forgive, I forget
         Life's hoard of regret—
         All the terror and pain
         Of the chafing chain.
         Grind on, O cities, grind:
         I leave you a blur behind.
I am lifted elate—the skies expand:
Here the world's heaped gold is a pile of sand.
Let them weary and work in their narrow walls:
I ride with the voices of waterfalls!
I swing on as one in a dream—I swing
Down the airy hollows, I shout, I sing!
The world is gone like an empty word:
My body's a bough in the wind, my heart a bird!

Reprinted by permission of the author. Copyright by Edwin Markham.

The Hills

Berton Braley

Berton Braley was born in 1882. He is a newspaper man, a poet, and a novelist. During the war he was a special correspondent in northern Europe.

Read this poem with a rugged grandeur akin to that of the mountains that are described. Note, however, the change in mood in the early part of the last stanza.

PARTNER, remember the hills?
The gray, barren, bleak old hills
We knew so well—
Not those gentle, placid slopes that swell
In lazy undulations, lush and green.
No; the real hills, the jagged crests,
The sharp and sheer-cut pinnacles of earth
That stand against the azure—gaunt, serene,
Careless of all our little worsts and bests,
Our sorrow and our mirth!

Partner, remember the hills?
Those snow-crowned, granite battlements of hills
We loved of old.
They stood so calm, inscrutable and cold,
Somehow it never seemed they cared at all
For you or me, our fortunes or our fall,
And yet we felt their thrall;
And ever and forever to the end
We shall not cease, my friend,
To hear their call.

Partner, remember the hills?
The grim and massive majesty of hills
That soared so far,
Seeming, at night, to scrape against a star.
Do you remember how we lay at night
(When the great herd had settled down to sleep)
And watched the moonshine—white
Against the peaks all garlanded with snow,
While soft and low
The night wind murmured in our ears—and so
We wrapped our blankets closer, looked again
At those great shadowy mountain-tops, and then
Sank gently to our deep
And quiet sleep?

Partner, remember the hills?
The real hills, the true hills.
Ah, I have tried
To brush the memory of them aside;
To learn to love
Those fresh, green hills the poets carol of;
But the old gray hills of barrenness still hold
My heart so much in thrall
That I forget the beauty all about,
The grass and flowers and all;
And just cry out
To take again the faint and wind-swept trail,
To see my naked mountains, shale and snow,
To feel again the hill-wind and to know
The spell that shall not fail.

Reprinted by permission of, and special arrangement with, Geo. H. Doran Company, from *Songs of the Workaday World.* Copyright, 1915.

Highmount

Louis Untermeyer

For biographical note concerning the author, see "The Laughers," page 88.

This exquisite poem may well test the imagination of the reader. Bring out the contrast between the restless impatience of the sea and the calm solidity of the hills. Do not forget the rhyme.

HILLS, you have answered the craving
    That spurred me to come;
You have opened your deep blue bosom
    And taken me home.

The sea had filled me with the stress
Of its own restlessness;
My voice was in that angry roll
Of passion beating upon the world.
The ground beneath me shifted; I was swirled
In an implacable flood that howled to see
Its breakers rising in me,
A torrent rushing through my soul,
And tearing things free.
I could not control
A monstrous impatience, a stubborn and vain
Repetition of madness and longing, of question and
    pain,
Driving me up to the brow of this hill—
Calling and questioning still.

And you—you smile
In ordered calm;

You wrap yourself in cloudy contemplation while
The winds go shouting their heroic psalm;
The streams press lovingly about your feet
And trees, like birds escaping from the heat,
Sit in great flocks and fold their broad green
    wings. . . .
A cow bell rings
Like a sound blurred by sleep,
Giving the silence a rhythm
That makes it twice as deep . . .
Somewhere a farm-hand sings . . .

And here you stand
Breasting the elemental sea,
And put forth an invisible hand
To comfort me.
Rooted in quiet confidence, you rise
Above the frantic and assailing years;
Your silent faith is louder than the cries;
The shattering fears
Break and subside when they encounter you.
You know their doubts, the desperate questions—
And the answers too.

    Hills, you are strong; and my burdens
        Are scattered like foam;
    You have opened your deep blue bosom
        And taken me home.

Reprinted by permission of the author, and by permission of, and special arrangement with, Henry Holt and Company.

May is Building Her House

Richard Le Gallienne

Richard Le Gallienne was born in Liverpool, January 20, 1866. He is a journalist and man of letters. He was educated at Liverpool College and has published numerous poems, sonnets, and essays.

This beautiful fancy should be rendered with tenderness and delight. There is much music in the rhyme, which should be fully developed. Paint each picture as vividly as possible without destroying the onward flow of the verse.

MAY is building her house. With apple blooms
  She is roofing over the glimmering rooms;
Of the oak and the beech hath she builded its beams,
  And spinning all day at her secret looms,
With arras of leaves each wind-swayed wall
She pictureth over, and peopleth it all
    With echoes and dreams,
    And singing of streams.

May is building her house. Of petal and blade,
Of the roots of the oak, is the flooring made,
  With a carpet of mosses and lichen and clover,
  Each small miracle over and over,
And tender, traveling green things strayed.

Her windows, the morning and evening star,
And her rustling doorways, ever ajar
    With the coming and going
    Of fair things blowing,
The thresholds of the four winds are.

May is building her house.   From the dust of things
She is making the songs and the flowers and the
       wings;
  From October's tossed and trodden gold
  She is making the young year out of the old;
    Yea: Out of winter's flying sleet
    She is making all the summer sweet,
    And the brown leaves spurned of November's
      feet
She is changing back again into spring's.

Reprinted by permission of the author and Harper and
Brothers, publishers of the author's works.

After Sunset

Grace Hazard Conkling

Grace Hazard Conkling was born in New York City. She entered
Smith College in 1899 and later studied music and languages in
Heidelberg and Paris. She married Roscoe Platt Conkling in
1905. She is teaching English in Smith College at the present
time, and contributes poems to a number of the leading magazines
of the country.

An effective oral interpretation of this intimate study of one of
Nature's most impressive phenomena requires slow rate, with
appropriate tone-color to depict the varying scenes and sentiments.

I HAVE an understanding with the hills
At evening, when the slanted radiance fills
Their hollows, and the great winds let them be,
And they are quiet and look down at me.
Oh, then I see the patience in their eyes
Out of the centuries that made them wise.
They lend me hoarded memory, and I learn
Their thoughts of granite and their whims of fern.

And why a dream of forests must endure
Though every tree be slain; and how the pure,
Invisible beauty has a word so brief
A flower can say it, or a shaken leaf,
But few may ever snare it in a song,
Though for the quest a life is not too long.
When the blue hills grow tender, when they pull
The twilight close with gesture beautiful,
And shadows are their garments, and the air
Deepens, and the wild veery is at prayer,
Their arms are strong around me; and I know
That somehow I shall follow when they go
To the still land beyond the evening star,
Where everlasting hills and valleys are,
And silence may not hurt us any more,
And terror shall be past, and grief and war.

Reprinted by permission of the author and Henry Holt
and Company.

A Dakota Wheat Field

Hamlin Garland

Hamlin Garland was born in West Salem, Wisconsin, on September 16, 1860. He is a novelist and dramatist. As a boy he worked on a farm and went to school, and later taught school in Illinois. He began to write stories about 1893.

Residents of states having expansive wheat fields will recognize how true to nature is the following beautiful description. The poem, especially in the second stanza, offers opportunity for the study of changes in rate to express changing scenes and emotions.

LIKE liquid gold the wheat field lies,
   A marvel of yellow and russet and green,
That ripples and runs, that floats and flies,

With the subtle shadows, the change, the sheen
   That play in the golden hair of a girl,—
      A ripple of amber—a flare
   Of light sweeping after—a curl
   In the hollows. Like swirling feet
      Of fairy waltzers, the colors run
      To the western sun
   Through the deeps of the ripening wheat.

Broad as the fleckless, soaring sky,
   Mysterious, fair as the moon-led sea,
The vast plain flames on the dazzled eye
   Under the fierce sun's alchemy.
      The slow hawk stoops
         To his prey in the deeps;
      The sunflower droops
         To the lazy wave; the wind sleeps.
      Then all in dazzling links and loops,
         A riot of shadow and shine,
         A glory of olive and amber and wine,
   To the westering sun the colors run
   Through the deeps of the ripening wheat.

O glorious land! My Western land,
   Outspread beneath the setting sun!
Once more amid your swells I stand,
   And cross your sod lands dry and dun.
I hear the jocund calls of men
   Who sweep amid the ripened grain,
With swift, stern reapers, once again.
      The evening splendor floods the plain:
         The crickets' chime

Makes pauseless rhyme,
And toward the sun
The splendid colors ramp and run
Before the wind's feet
In the wheat!

Reprinted by permission of the author.

Landscapes

Louis Untermeyer

For biographical note concerning the author, see "The Laughers,"
page 88.

The varied scenes and objects so beautifully portrayed in this
poem, together with the contrasting picture toward the close, should
be clearly shown by due emphasis, while the rhythm of the whole
should not be neglected.

THE rain was over, and the brilliant air
Made every little blade of grass appear
Vivid and startling—everything was there
With sharpened outlines, eloquently clear,
As though one saw it in a crystal sphere.

The rusty sumac with its struggling spires;
The golden-rod with all its million fires;
(A million torches swinging in the wind)
A single poplar, marvelously thinned,
Half like a naked body, half like a sword;
Clouds, like the haughty banners of the Lord;
A group of pansies with their shrewish faces,
Little old ladies cackling over laces;
The quaint, unhurried road that curved so well;
The prim petunias with their rich, rank smell;

The lettuce-birds, the creepers in the field—
How bountifully were they all revealed!
How arrogantly each one seemed to thrive—
So frank and strong, so radiantly alive!

And over all the morning-minded earth
There seemed to spread a sharp and kindling mirth,
Piercing the stubborn stones until I saw
The toad face heaven without shame or awe,
The ant confront the stars, and every weed
Grow proud as though it bore a royal seed;
While all the things that die and decompose
Sent forth their bloom as richly as the rose. . . .
Oh, what a liberal power that made them thrive
And keep the very dirt that died, alive!

And now I saw the slender willow-tree,
No longer calm or drooping listlessly,
Letting its languid branches sway and fall
As though it danced in some sad ritual;
But rather like a young athletic girl,
Fearless and gay, her hair all out of curl,
And flying in the wind—her head thrown back,
Her arms flung up, her garments flowing slack,
And all her rushing spirits running over. . . .
What made a sober tree seem such a rover—
Or made the staid and stalwart apple-trees,
That stood for years knee-deep in velvet peace,
Turn all their fruit to little worlds of flame,
And burn the trembling orchard there below?
What lit the heart of every golden-glow—
Oh, why was nothing weary, dull, or tame? . . .

Beauty it was, and keen, compassionate mirth
That drives the vast and energetic earth.

And, with abrupt and visionary eyes,
I saw the huddled tenements arise.
Here where the merry clover danced and shone
Sprang agonies of iron and stone;
There, where the green Silence laughed or stood
    enthralled,
Cheap music blared and evil alleys sprawled.
The roaring avenues, the shrieking mills;
Brothels and prisons on those kindly hills—
The menace of these things swept over me;
A threatening, unconquerable sea. . . .

A stirring landscape and a generous earth!
Freshening courage and benevolent mirth—
And then the city, like a hideous sore. . . .
Good God, and what is all this beauty for?

Reprinted by permission of the author and Henry Holt
and Company.

Catalog of Lovely Things

Richard Le Gallienne

For biographical mention of Richard Le Gallienne see **"May is**
Building Her House," page 29.

Do you think that the author has omitted anything in **this**
"Catalog of Lovely Things"? In any event, you will need to **go**
slowly in rendering these lines, in order that the things successively
mentioned may be duly appreciated and impressed.

I would make a list against the evil days
    Of lovely things to hold in memory:

First, I set down my lady's lovely face,
    For earth hath no such lovely thing as she;
    And next I add, to bear her company,
The great-eyed virgin star that morning brings;
    Then the wild rose upon its little tree—
So runs my catalog of lovely things.

The enchanted dogwood, with its ivory trays;
    The water-lily in its sanctuary
Of reeded pools; and dew-drenched lilac sprays:
    For these, of all fair flowers, the fairest be.
    Next write I down the great name of the sea,
Lonely in greatness as the names of kings;
    Then the young moon that hath us all in fee—
So runs my catalog of lovely things.

Imperial sunsets that in crimson blaze
    Along the hills; and, fairer still to me,
The fireflies dancing in a netted maze
    Woven of twilight and tranquillity;
    Shakespeare and Virgil—their high poesy;
And a great ship, splendid with snowy wings,
    Voyaging on into Eternity—
So runs my catalog of lovely things.

ENVOI

Prince, not the gold bars of thy treasury,
Not all thy jeweled scepters, crowns, and rings,
Are worth the honeycomb of the wild bee—
So runs my catalog of lovely things.

Reprinted by permission of the author and Harper and Brothers, the publishers of the author's works.

The Winter Scene

Bliss Carman

Bliss Carman was born at Fredericton, New Brunswick, April 15, 1861. He was educated at the University of New Brunswick, the University of Edinburgh, and Harvard. He studied law and was engaged in editorial work, but since 1894 has devoted himself entirely to literary pursuits. He is the author of many volumes of prose and verse.

The following blank-verse description of a northern winter runs true to form, having a more expansive background than the more localized and specific descriptions found in Whittier's "Snow Bound." If the reader keenly visualizes the scenes described, the vocal rendition will offer no special difficulty.

I

THE rutted roads are all like iron; the skies
Are keen and brilliant; only the oak-leaves cling
In the bare woods, or hardy bitter-sweet;
Drivers have put their sheepskin jackets on;
And all the ponds are sealed with sheeted ice
That rings with stroke of skate and hockey-stick,
Or in the twilight cracks with running whoop.
Bring in the logs of oak and hickory,
And make an ample blaze on the wide hearth.
Now is the time, with winter o'er the world,
For books and friends and yellow candle-light,
And timeless lingering by the settling fire,
While all the shuddering stars are keen and cold.

2

Out of the silent portal of the hours,
When frosts are come and all the hosts put on
Their burnished gear to march across the night
And o'er a darkened earth in splendor whine,

Slowly above the world Orion wheels
His glittering square, while on the shadowy hill
And throbbing like a sea-light through the dusk,
Great Sirius rises in his flashing blue.
Lord of the winter night, august and pure,
Returning year on year untouched by time,
To kindle faith with thy immortal fire,
There are no hurts that beauty cannot ease,
No ills that love cannot at last repair,
In the courageous progress of the soul

3

Russet and white and gray is the oak wood
In the great snow. Still from the North it comes,
Whispering, settling, sifting through the trees,
O'erloading branch and twig. The road is lost.
Clearing and meadow, stream and ice-bound pond
Are made once more a trackless wilderness
In the white hush where not a creature stirs;
And the pale sun is blotted from the sky.
In that strange twilight the lone traveller halts
To listen while the stealthy snowflakes fall.
And then far off toward the Stamford shore,
Where through the storm the coastwise liners go,
Faint and recurrent on the muddled air,
A foghorn booming through the smother,—hark!

4

When the day changed and the mad wind died
    down,

The powdery drifts that all day long had blown
Across the meadows and the open fields,
Or whirled like diamond dust in the bright sun,
Settled to rest, and for a tranquil hour
The lengthening bluish shadows on the snow
Stole down the orchard slope, and a rose light
Flooded the earth with glory and with peace,
Then in the west behind the cedars black
The sinking sun made red the winter dusk
With sudden flare along the snowy ridge,—
Like a rare masterpiece by Hokusai,
Where on a background gray, with flaming breath
The crimson dragon dies in dusky gold.

Reprinted by permission of the author.

Deserted

Madison Cawein

Madison Cawein was born at Louisville, Kentucky in 1865, and died in 1915. He began writing at twenty-two years of age and continued until his death. He was preëminently a poet of Nature.

Picture yourself abroad on such a night as the poet here describes. See the old, deserted house. Strive to reproduce in yourself the emotions you would feel when contemplating it. The pitch is low, the movement slow.

THE old house leans upon a tree
    Like some old man upon a staff;
The night wind in its ancient porch
    Sounds like a hollow laugh.

The heaven is wrapped in flying clouds
    As grandeur cloaks itself in gray:

The starlight, fluttering in and out,
    Glints like a lanthorn ray.

The dark is full of whispers.   Now
    A fox-hound howls: and through the night,
Like some old ghost from out its grave,
    The moon comes misty white.

Reprinted by permission of, and special arrangement with, E. P. Dutton and Company.

Down the Mississippi

John Gould Fletcher

John Gould Fletcher was born at Little Rock, Arkansas, in 1886. He was educated at Harvard, but soon after went to England, where he has since spent most of his time. His early works were highly fanciful, but "Lincoln" and his later works are strong and moving. His works include "Goblins and Pagodas," published by Houghton Mifflin and Co., "The Tree of Life," published by Chatto and Windus, London, and "Breakers and Granite," published by The Macmillan Company, New York.

This composition might well be styled a "poem of pictures and moods." The moods are the result of the pictures. Let the reader see the different scenes vividly and let them work their magic upon his "bodily texture." Notice a certain unity, too, through the entire poem. Do not neglect the sublimity of the last lines.

Embarkation

DULL masses of dense green,
The forests range their sombre platforms.
Between them silently, like a spirit,
The river finds its own mysterious path.

Loosely the river sways out, backward, forward,
Always fretting the outer side;

Shunning the invisible focus of each crescent,
Seeking to spread into shining loops over fields:

Like an enormous serpent, dilating, uncoiling,
Displaying a broad scaly back of earth-smeared
  gold;
Swaying out sinuously between the dull motionless
  forests,
As molten metal might glide down the lip of a
  vase of dark bronze.

Heat

As if the sun had trodden down the sky,
Until no more it holds air for us, but only humid
  vapor,
The heat, pressing upon earth with irresistible
  languor,
Turns all the solid forest into half-liquid smudge.

The heavy clouds, like cargo-boats, strain slowly
  up 'gainst its current;
And the flickering of the heat haze is like the
  churning of ten thousand paddles
Against the heavy horizon, pale blue and utterly
  windless,
Whereon the sun hangs motionless, a brassy disk
  of flame.

Full Moon

Flinging its arc of silver bubbles, quickly shifts the
  moon

From side to side of us as we go down its path;
I sit on the deck at midnight, and watch it slipping
    and sliding,
Under my tilted chair, like a thin film of spilt water.

It is weaving a river of light to take the place of this
    river—
A river where we shall drift all night, then come
    to rest in its shallows.
And then I shall wake from my drowsiness and look
    down from some dim tree-top
Over white lakes of cotton, like moon-fields on
    every side.

The Moon's Orchestra

When the moon lights up
Its dull red camp-fire through the trees;
And floats out, like a white balloon,
Into the blue cup of the night, borne by a casual
    breeze;
The moon-orchestra then begins to stir:
Jiggle of fiddles commence their crazy dance in the
    darkness;
Crickets churr
Against the stark reiteration of the rusty flutes
    which frogs
Puff at from rotted logs
In the swamp.
And the moon begins her dance of frozen pomp
Over the lightly quivering floor of the flat and
    mournful river.

Her white feet slightly twist and swirl—
She is a mad girl
In an old unlit ball-room,
Whose walls, half-guessed-at through the gloom,
Are hung with the rusty crape of stark black
　　cypresses,
Which show, through gaps and tatters, red stains
　　half hidden away.

The Stevedores

Frieze of warm bronze that glides with cat-like
　　movements
Over the gang-plank poised and yet awaiting—
The sinewy thudding rhythms of forty shuffling
　　feet
Falling like muffled drum-beats on the stillness:
　　　　　Oh, roll the cotton down—
　　　　　Roll, roll, the cotton down!
　　　　　From the further side of Jordan,
　　　　　Oh, roll the cotton down!
And the river waits,
The river listens,
Chuckling with little banjo-notes that break with a
　　plop on the stillness.
And by the low dark shed that holds the heavy
　　freights,
Two lonely cypress trees stand up and point with
　　stiffened fingers
Far southward where a single chimney stands aloof
　　in the sky.

Night Landing

After the whistle's roar has bellowed and shuddered,
Shaking the sleeping town and the somnolent river,
The deep-toned floating of the pilot's bell
Suddenly warns the engines.
They pause like heart-beats that abruptly stop:
The shore glides to us, in a wide low curve.
And then—supreme revelation of the river—
The tackle is loosed, the long gang-plank swings
    outwards;   •
And poised at the end of it, half naked beneath the
    searchlight,
A blue-black negro with gleaming teeth waits for
his chance to leap.

The Silence

There is a silence which I carry about with me
    always—
A silence perpetual, for it is self-created;
A silence of heat, of water, of unchecked fruit-
    fulness,
Through which each year the heavy harvests bloom,
    and burst, and fall.

Deep, matted green silence of my South,
Often, within the push and the scorn of great cities,
I have seen that mile-wide waste of water swaying
    out to you,
And on its current glimmering I am going to the sea.

There is a silence I have achieved—I have walked
    beyond its threshold.
I know it is without horizons, boundless, fathom-
    less, perfect.
And some day, maybe, far away,
I shall curl up in it at last and sleep an endless sleep.

Reprinted by permission of, and by special arrange-
ment with, The Macmillan Company. Copyrighted by The
Macmillan Company.

A Vagabond Song

Bliss Carman

For biographical note concerning the author, see "The Winter
Scene," page 37.

This is truly a song, but do not fail to reveal the emotions
stirred by the flitting visions of autumn.

THERE is something in the autumn that is native to
    my blood—
Touch of manner, hint of mood;
And my heart is like a rhyme,
With the yellow and the purple and the crimson
    keeping time.

The scarlet of the maples can shake me like a cry
Of bugles going by,
And my lonely spirit thrills
To see the frosty asters like a smoke upon the hills.

There is something in October sets the gypsy blood
    astir;

We must rise and follow her,
    When from every hill of flame
    She calls and calls each vagabond by name.

Reprinted by permission of, and special arrangement with, Small, Maynard and Co.

God's World

Edna St. Vincent Millay

Edna St. Vincent Millay was born at Camden, Maine, and was educated at Vassar College. Some of her published volumes are "Renascence and Other Poems," "Second April," both published by Mitchell Kennerley, New York, and "Some Figs from Thistles," published by Frank Shay, New York.

Seldom does such passion as this succeed in revealing itself in verse. Restraint must characterize any reading of this poem, but such a restraint as threatens every moment to break out of bounds. A holding back upon the beginning of the words, and an impassioned emphasis upon the latter parts of them may help the reader.

O WORLD, I cannot hold thee close enough!
    Thy winds, thy wide gray skies!
    Thy mists that roll and rise!
Thy woods this autumn day, that ache and sag
And all but cry with color! That gaunt crag
To crush! To lift the lean of that black bluff!
World, World, I cannot get thee close enough!

Long have I known a glory in it all,
    But never knew I this;
    Here such a passion is
As stretcheth me apart,—Lord, I do fear
Thou'st made the world too beautiful this year;
My soul is all but out of me,—let fall
No burning leaf; prithee, let no bird call.

Reprinted by permission of Mitchell Kennerley.

Ellis Park

Helen Hoyt

Helen Hoyt (Mrs. W. W. Lyman) was born at Norwalk, Conn., and educated at Barnard College, where she was graduated in 1909. She taught for a while in the Middle West, later joining the staff of *Poetry* and becoming Associate Editor. She now resides at St. Helena, Calif.

Let the tone of this poem be that of affection,—almost childish tenderness.

LITTLE park that I pass through,
I carry off a piece of you
Every morning hurrying down
To my work-day in the town;
Carry you for country there
To make the city ways more fair.
I take your trees,
And your breeze,
Your greenness,
Your cleanness,
Some of your shade, some of your sky,
Some of your calm as I go by;
Your flowers to trim
The pavements grim;
Your space for room in the jostled street,
And grass for carpet to my feet.
Your fountains take, and sweet bird calls,
To sing me from my office walls;
All that I can see
I carry off with me.
But you never miss my theft,
So much treasure you have left.
As I find you, fresh at morning,
So I find you, home returning—

Nothing lacking from your grace.
All your riches wait in place
For me to borrow
On the morrow.

Do you hear this praise of you,
Little park that I pass through?

Reprinted by permission of the author.

In Lady Street

John Drinkwater

John Drinkwater, the author of the famous play *Abraham Lincoln*, was born in 1882. He has published essays, poems, and plays, and has been general manager of the Birmingham (England) Repertory Theatre. Most of his poems are meditative in mood.

In reading this poem be sure to reveal the ugliness of the scene in the opening lines, and then transform that ugliness into beauty worthy of admiration. Low tones will mark the opening of the poem with traces of the guttural quality. Later the tone is higher and brighter, and abounds in waves of wonder and beauty.

ALL day long the traffic goes
In Lady Street by dingy rows
Of sloven houses, tattered shops—
Fried fish, old clothes and fortune-tellers—
Tall trams on silver-shining rails,
With grinding wheels and swaying tops,
And lorries with their corded bales,
And screeching cars. "Buy, buy!" the sellers
Of rags and bones and sickening meat
Cry all day long in Lady Street.

And when the sunshine has its way
In Lady Street, then all the gray

Dull desolation grows in state
More dull and gray and desolate,
And the sun is a shamefast thing,
A lord not comely-housed, a god
Seeing what gods must blush to see,
A song where it is ill to sing,
And each gold ray despiteously
Lies like a gold ironic rod.
Yet one gray man in Lady Street
Looks for the sun. He never bent
Life to his will, his traveling feet
Have scaled no cloudy continent,
Nor has the sickle-hand been strong.
He lies in Lady Street; a bed,
Four cobwebbed walls. But all day long
A tune is singing in his head
Of youth in Gloucester lanes. He hears
The wind among the barley-blades,
The tapping of the woodpeckers
On the smooth beeches, thistle-spades
Slicing the sinewy roots; he sees
The hooded filberts in the copse
Beyond the loaded orchard trees,
The netted avenues of hops;
He smells the honeysuckle thrown
Along the hedge. He lives alone,
Alone—yet not alone, for sweet
Are Gloucester lanes in Lady Street.

Ay, Gloucester lanes. For down below
The cobwebbed room this gray man plies

A trade, a colored trade.   A show
Of many-colored merchandise
Is in his shop.   Brown filberts there
And apples red with Gloucester air,
And cauliflowers he keeps, and round
Smooth marrows grown on Gloucester ground,
Fat cabbages and yellow plums,
And gaudy brave chrysanthemums.
And times a glossy pheasant lies
Among his store, not Tyrian dyes
More rich than are the neck-feathers;
And times a prize of violets,
Or dewy mushrooms satin-skinned,
And times an unfamiliar wind
Robbed of its woodland favor stirs
Gay daffodils this gray man sets
Among his treasure.

All day long
In Lady Street the traffic goes
By dingy houses, desolate rows
Of shops that stare like hopeless eyes.
Day long the sellers cry their cries,
The fortune-tellers tell no wrong
Of lives that know not any right,
And drift, that has not even the will
To drift, toils through the day until
The wage of sleep is won at night.
But this gray man heeds not all
The hell of Lady Street.   His stall
Of many-colored merchandise
Makes a shining paradise,

As all day long chrysanthemums
He sells, and red and yellow plums
And cauliflowers.   In that one spot
Of Lady Street the sun is not
Ashamed to shine, and send a rare
Shower of color through the air,
The gray man says.

Reprinted by permission of, and by special arrangement with, Houghton Mifflin Company.

The Steam Shovel

Eunice Tietjens

Eunice Tietjens was born in Chicago in 1884. Her maiden name was Eunice Hammond, but she married Paul Tietjens, the composer, in 1904. She has been an associate editor of *Poetry*, and during the war was correspondent to the Chicago *Daily News*. In 1920 she married Cloyd Head, the writer.

Read this poem with great restrained force. Use low pitch and a certain plunging utterance that takes its form from the action of the steam shovel or the earlier monster. Note the change in mood, however, toward the end.

BENEATH my window in a city street
A monster lairs, a creature huge and grim
And only half believed: the strength of him—
Steel-strung and fit to meet
The strength of earth—
Is mighty as men's dreams that conquer force.
Steam belches from him. He is the new birth
Of old Behemoth, late-sprung from the source
Whence Grendel sprang, and all the monster clan
Dead for an age, now born again of man.

The iron head,
Set on a monstrous jointed neck,
Glides here and there, lifts, settles on the red
Moist floor, with nose dropped in the dirt, at beck
Of some incredible control.
He snorts, and pauses couchant for a space;
Then slowly lifts, and tears the gaping hole
Yet deeper in earth's flank.   A sudden race
Of loosened earth and pebbles trickles there
Like blood-drops in a wound.
But he, the monster, swings his load around,—
Weightless it seems as air—
His mammoth jaw
Drops widely open with a rasping sound,
And all the red earth vomits from his maw.

O thwarted monster, born at man's decree,
A lap-dog dragon, eating from his hand
And doomed to fetch and carry at command,
Have you no longing ever to be free?
In warm electric days to run a-muck,
Ranging like some mad dinosaur,
Your fiery heart at war
With this strange world, the city's restless ruck,
Where all drab things that toil, save you alone,
Have life;
And you the semblance only, and the strife?
Do you not yearn to rip the roots of stone
Of these great piles men build,
And hurl them down with shriek of shattered steel,
Scorning your own sure doom, so you may feel,

You too, the lust with which your fathers killed?
Or is your soul in very deed so tame,
The blood of Grendel watered to a gruel,
That you are well content
With heart of flame
Thus placidly to chew your cud of fuel
And toil in peace for man's aggrandizement?

Poor helpless creature of a half-grown god,
Blind of yourself and impotent!
At night,
When your forerunners, sprung from quicker sod,
Would range through primal woods, hot on the
    scent,
Or wake the stars with amorous delight,
You stand, a soiled, unwieldy mass of steel,
Black in the arc-light, modern as your name,
Dead and unsouled and trite;
Till I must feel
A quick creator's pity for your shame:
That man, who made you and who gave so much,
Yet cannot give the last transforming touch;
That with the work he cannot give the wage—
For day, no joy of night,
For toil, no ecstasy of primal rage.

Reprinted from *Body and Raiment* by Eunice Tietjens, by permission of Alfred A. Knopf, Inc., authorized publishers.

Caliban in the Coal Mines

Louis Untermeyer

For biographical note concerning the author, see "Landscapes," page 33.

Do not read this poem in a weak, complaining way. Rather let it be the medium for heroic resignation. Do not neglect the magnificent emotional outburst in the last two lines.

God, we don't like to complain—
 We know that the mine is no lark—
But—there's the pools from the rain;
 But—there's the cold and the dark.

God, You don't know what it is—
 You, in Your well-lighted sky—
Watching the meteors whizz;
 Warm, with the sun always by.

God, if You had but the moon
 Stuck in Your cap for a lamp,
Even You'd tire of it soon,
 Down in the dark and the damp.

Nothing but blackness above
 And nothing that moves but the cars. . . .
God, if You wish for our love,
 Fling us a handful of stars!

From *Challenge* by Louis Untermeyer. Copyright, 1920, by Harcourt, Brace, and Howe, Inc.

The Stone

Wilfrid Wilson Gibson

Wilfrid Wilson Gibson was born at Hexam, England, in 1878. His early work was sentimental and romantic, but in his later works he has set forth boldly the life of the working people. His later books include "The Stonefolds," published by the Samurai Press, London, "Daily Bread," published by Elkin Mathews, London, and "Fires," also published by Elkin Mathews and The Macmillan Company, New York.

Great restraint should characterize the reading of this poem. All the varying moods are felt under the spell of the great master-mood of tragedy.

"And will you cut a stone for him,
To set above his head?
And will you cut a stone for him—
A stone for him?" she said.

Three days before, a splintered rock
Had struck her lover dead—
Had struck him in the quarry dead,
Where, careless of the warning call,
He loitered, while the shot was fired—
A lively stripling, brave and tall,
And sure of all his heart desired. . . .
A flash, a shock,
A rumbling fall. . . .
And, broken 'neath the broken rock,
A lifeless heap, with face of clay,
And still as any stone he lay,
With eyes that saw the end of all.

I went to break the news to her;
And I could hear my own heart beat
With dread of what my lips might say.
But some poor fool had sped before;
And flinging wide her father's door,
Had blurted out the news to her,
Had struck her lover dead for her,
Had struck the girl's heart dead in her,
Had struck life, lifeless, at a word,
And dropped it at her feet:
Then hurried on his witless way,
Scarce knowing she had heard.

And when I came, she stood, alone,
A woman, turned to stone:
And, though no word at all she said,
I knew that all was known.

Because her heart was dead,
She did not sigh nor moan.
His mother wept:
She could not weep.
Her lover slept:
She could not sleep.
Three days, three nights,
She did not stir:
Three days, three nights,
Were one to her,
Who never closed her eyes
From sunset to sunrise,
From dawn to evenfall:

Her tearless, staring eyes,
That seeing naught, saw all.

The fourth night when I came from work,
I found her at my door.
"And will you cut a stone for him?"
She said and spoke no more:
But followed me, as I went in,
And sank upon a chair;
And fixed her gray eyes on my face,
With still, unseeing stare.
And, as she waited patiently,
I could not bear to feel
Those still, gray eyes that followed me,
Those eyes that plucked the heart from me,
Those eyes that sucked the breath from me
And curdled the warm blood in me,
Those eyes that cut me to the bone,
And pierced my marrow like cold steel.

And so I rose, and sought a stone;
And cut it, smooth and square:
And, as I worked, she sat and watched,
Beside me, in her chair.
Night after night, so still and white,
And like a ghost she came;
And sat beside me in her chair;
And watched with eyes aflame.

She eyed each stroke;
And hardly stirred:

She never spoke
A single word:
And not a sound or murmur broke
The quiet, save the mallet-stroke.
With still eyes ever on my hands,
With eyes that seemed to burn my hands,
My wincing, overwearied hands,
She watched, with bloodless lips apart,
And silent, indrawn breath:
And every stroke my chisel cut,
Death cut still deeper in her heart:
The two of us were chiseling,
Together, I and death.

And when at length the job was done,
And I had laid the mallet by,
As if, at last, her peace were won,
She breathed his name; and, with a sigh,
Passed slowly through the open door:
And never crossed my threshold more.

Next night I laboured late, alone,
To cut her name upon the stone.

Reprinted by permission of, and by special arrangement with, The Macmillan Company. Copyrighted by The Macmillan Company.

On a Subway Express

Chester Firkins

Chester Firkins was born at Minneapolis, Minnesota, in 1882. He was educated at the University of Minnesota, and soon after took up journalism, being at his death in 1915, on the staff of the New York *American*. He wrote short stories as well as verse.

Anyone who has ridden in a subway express will appreciate the imaginative touch that has made the sordid ride a worshipful communion with God. If the poem is treated seriously it can be made to appeal to the imagination with great power.

I, WHO have lost the stars, the sod,
    For chilling pave and cheerless light,
Have made my meeting-place with God
    A new and nether Night—

Have found a fane where thunder fills
    Loud caverns, tremulous;—and these
Atone me for my reverend hills
    And moonlit silences.

A figment in the crowded dark,
    Where men sit muted by the roar,
I ride upon the whirring spark
    Beneath the city's floor.

In this dim firmament, the stars
    Whirl by in blazing files and tiers;
Kin meteors graze our flying bars,
    Amid the spinning spheres.

Speed! speed! until the quivering rails
    Flash silver where the headlight gleams,

As when on lakes the moon impales
    The waves upon its beams.

Life throbs about me, yet I stand
    Outgazing on majestic power;
Death rides with me, on either hand,
    In my communion hour.

You that 'neath country skies can pray,
    Scoff not at me—the city clod!
My only respite of the day
    Is this wild ride—with God.

Songs for My Mother

Anna Hempstead Branch

Anna Hempstead Branch was born at New London, Conn. She entered Smith College in 1897 and later attended the American Academy of Dramatic Art. She won the first of the Century prizes awarded to college graduates for the best poem with "The Road 'Twixt Heaven and Hell." She has since written a number of poems and some prose and contributes to the leading magazines.

The tone of the following two selections is tender and affectionate. The time is even and moderately slow, for the most part. There is an atmosphere of reminiscence about these poems. The force employed in rendering the lines should be gentle. The pitch is moderately low. These selections should not be delivered in a childish manner, although the manner of the adult is *tinged* with childish inflections.

I

Her Hands

My mother's hands are cool and fair,
    They can do anything.

Delicate mercies hide them there,
  Like flowers in the spring.

When I was small and could not sleep,
  She used to come to me,
And with my cheek upon her hand
  How sure my rest would be!

For everything she ever touched
  Of beautiful and fine,
Their memories, living in her hands,
  Would warm that sleep of mine.

Her hands remember how they played
  One time in meadow streams,—
And all the flickering song and shade
  Of water took my dreams.

Swift through her haunted fingers pass
  Memories of garden things;—
I dipped my face in flowers and grass
  And sounds of hidden wings.

One time she touched the cloud that kissed
  Brown pastures bleak and far;—
I leaned my cheek into a mist
  And thought I was a star.

All this was very long ago
  And I am grown; but yet
The hand that lured my slumber so
  I never can forget.

For still when drowsiness comes on
  It seems so soft and cool,
Shaped happily beneath my cheek,
  Hollow and beautiful!

2

Her Words

My mother has the prettiest tricks
  Of words and words and words.
Her talk comes out as smooth and sleek
  As breasts of singing birds.

She shapes her speech all silver fine
  Because she loves it so.
And her own eyes begin to shine
  To hear her stories grow.

And if she goes to make a call
  Or out to take a walk,
We leave our work when she returns
  And run to hear her talk.

We had not dreamed these things were so
  Of sorrow and of mirth.
Her speech is as a thousand eyes
  Through which we see the earth.

God wove a web of loveliness,
  Of clouds and stars and birds,
But made not anything at all
  So beautiful as words.

They shine around our simple earth
   With golden shadowings,
And every common thing they touch
   Is exquisite with wings.

There's nothing poor and nothing small
   But is made fair with them.
They are the hands of living faith
   That touch the garment's hem.

They are as fair as bloom or air,
   They shine like any star,
And I am rich who learned from her
   How beautiful they are.

Reprinted by permission of, and by special arrangement with, Houghton Mifflin Company, the owners of the copyright.

Roofs

Joyce Kilmer

Joyce Kilmer was born in New Brunswick, New Jersey, in 1886. He was educated at Columbia University. He was killed in action during the second Battle of the Marne, July 30, 1918. He is the author of several volumes of prose and verse.

This eloquent plea for home should be read in medium rate and with sustained earnestness and sympathy. Remember that *home* is the key-word throughout. A very fine effect may be obtained by dwelling upon and bringing out with increasing emphasis the repetition of "homes" in the fifth line from the last.

THE road is wide and the stars are out and the
      breath of the night is sweet,
And this is the time when wanderlust should seize
      upon my feet.

But I'm glad to turn from the open road and the
    starlight on my face,
And to leave the splendor of out-of-doors for a
    human dwelling-place.
I never have seen a vagabond who really liked to
    roam
All up and down the streets of the world and not
    have a home;
The tramp who slept in your barn last night and
    left at break of day
Will wander only until he finds another place to
    stay.
A gypsy man will sleep in his cart with canvas
    overhead,
Or else he'll go into his tent when it is time for
    bed.
He'll sit on the grass and take his ease so long as
    the sun is high,
But when it is dark he wants a roof to keep away
    the sky.
If you call a gypsy a vagabond, I think you do him
    wrong,
For he never goes a-traveling but he takes his home
    along.
And the only reason a road is good, as every
    wanderer knows,
Is just because of the homes, the homes to which
    it goes.
They say that life is a highway and its milestones
    are the years,
And now and then there's a toll-gate where you buy
    your way with tears.

It's a rough road and a steep road and it stretches
    broad and far,
But at last it leads to a golden Town where golden
    Houses are.

From *Joyce Kilmer: Poems, Essays, and Letters,*
edited by R. C. Holliday. Copyright 1914, by George H.
Doran Company, Publishers.

Piano

David Herbert Lawrence

David Herbert Lawrence was born in 1885. He is an English
poet, and is noted for his intense passion and emotion. Louis
Untermeyer in his "Modern American and British Poetry," says of
him: "As a poet he is often caught in the net of his own emo-
tions; his passion thickens his utterance and distorts his rhythms,
which sometimes seem purposely harsh and bitter-flavored. But
within his range he is as powerful as he is poignant." Among his
books of poetry are "Amores" and "Look! We Have Come
Through," published by B. W. Huebsch, Inc., New York, and "New
Poems," published by Martin Secher, London.

This delicate poem should be rendered delicately. Begin softly
and drift into affection and reverie. In the last stanza there is
an emotional revulsion at the music of the present singer, followed
by a complete capitulation to grief.

SOFTLY, in the dusk, a woman is singing to me;
Taking me back down the vista of years, till I see
A child sitting under the piano, in the boom of the
    tingling strings,
And pressing the small, poised feet of a mother who
    smiles as she sings.

In spite of myself, the insidious mastery of song
Betrays me back, till the heart of me weeps to
    belong

To the old Sunday evenings at home, with winter
    outside
And hymns in the cosy parlor, the tinkling piano
    our guide.

So now it is vain for the singer to burst into
    clamor
With the great black *piano appassionato.* The
    glamour
Of childish days is upon me, my manhood is cast
Down in the flood of remembrance, I weep like a
    child for the past.

Reprinted by permission of, and by special arrange-
ment with, B. W. Huebsch, Inc., New York. Copyrighted.

Autumn

Jean Starr Untermeyer

(To My Mother)

Jean Starr Untermeyer was born at Zanesville, Ohio, in 1886.
She was educated at Putnam Seminary, Zanesville, and Columbia
University, New York. She married Louis Untermeyer, the poet,
in 1907. She excels in speaking of ordinary things in a poetic
way. Her two published volumes are "Growing Pains" and
"Dreams out of Darkness," both published by B. W. Huebsch,
Inc., New York.

Rarely has the picture of the home life of the preceding genera-
tion been painted so clearly as in this poem. Linger over each
separate picture with affection, and if emotion bubbles up in the
closing lines, do not crush it out, yet keep it under control.

How memory cuts away the years,
And how clean the picture comes
Of autumn days, brisk and busy;
Charged with keen sunshine,

And you, stirred with activity,
The spirit of those energetic days!

There was our back yard,
So plain and stripped of green,
With even the weeds carefully pulled away
From the crooked red bricks that made the walk,
And the earth on either side so black.
Autumn and dead leaves burning in the sharp air,
And winter comforts coming in like a pageant,
I shall not forget them:—
Great jars laden with the raw green of pickles,
Standing in a solemn row across the back of the
    porch,
Exhaling the pungent dill;
And in the very center of the yard,
You, tending the great catsup kettle of gleaming
    copper,
Where fat, red tomatoes bobbed up and down
Like jolly monks in a drunken dance.
And there were bland banks of cabbage that came
    by the wagon-load,
Soon to be cut into delicate ribbons
Only to be crushed by the heavy, wooden stompers.
Such feathery whiteness—to come to kraut!
And after, there were grapes that hid their bright-
    ness
Under a gray dust,
Then gushed thrilling, purple blood over the fire;
And enameled crab-apples that tricked with their
    fragrance
But were bitter to taste.

And there were spicy plums and ill-shaped quinces,
And long string beans floating in pans of clear
    water
Like slim, green fishes.
And there was fish itself,
Salted, silver herring from the city. . . .

And you moved among these mysteries,
Absorbed and smiling and sure;
Stirring, tasting, measuring,
With the precision of a ritual.
I like to think of you in your years of power—
You, now so shaken and so powerless—
High priestess of your home!

Reprinted by permission of, and by special arrangement with, B. W. Huebsch, Inc., New York. Copyrighted.

The Two Houses

Thomas Hardy

Thomas Hardy is an English writer, born in 1840. He first wrote novels, among them "Tess of the D'Urbervilles," and did not take up poetry until he was nearly sixty. His collected poems were published by The Macmillan Company, New York, in 1919.

This poem may be read as direct conversation, yet there must be something of dignity and solitude and deep philosophy in the manner of its rendering.

In the heart of night,
    When farers were not near,
The left house said to the house on the right,
"I have marked your rise, O smart newcomer here!"

Said the right, cold-eyed:
"Newcomer here I am,
Hence haler than you with your cracked old hide,
Loose casements, wormy beams, and doors that
     jam.

"Modern my wood,
My hangings fair of hue;
While my windows open as they should
And water-pipes thread all my chambers through.

"Your gear is gray,
Your face wears furrows untold."
"Yours might," mourned the other, "if you held,
     brother,
The Presences from aforetime that I hold.

"You have not known
Men's lives, deaths, toils, and teens;
You are but a heap of stick and stone:
A new house has no sense of the have-beens.

"Void as a drum
You stand: I am packed with these;
Though, strangely, living dwellers who come
See not the phantoms all my substance sees!

"Visible in the morning
Stand they, when dawn crawls in;
Visible at night; yet hint or warning
Of these thin elbowers few of the inmates win.

"Babes new brought forth
   Obsess my rooms; straight-stretched
 Lank corpses, ere outborne to earth;
Yes, throng they as when first from the void up-
             fetched!

"Dancers and singers
   Throb in me now as once;
 Rich-noted throats and gossamered flingers
Of heels; the learned in love-lore, and the dunce.

"Note here within
   The bridegroom and the bride,
 Who smile and greet their friends and kin,
And down my stairs depart for tracts untried.

"Where such inbe,
   A dwelling's character
 Takes theirs, and a vague semblancy
To them in all its limbs and light and atmosphere.

"Yet the blind folk,
   My tenants, who come and go
 In the flesh mid these, with souls unwoke,
Of such sylph-like surrounders do not know."

"—Will the day come,"
   Said the new-built, awestruck, faint,
 "When I shall lodge shades dim and dumb,
And with such spectral guests become acquaint?"

"—That will it, boy;
  Such shades will people thee,
  Each in his misery, irk, or joy,
And print on thee their presences as on me!"

Reprinted by permission of, and by special arrange-
ment with, The Macmillan Company. Copyrighted by The
Macmillan Company.

The Chaperon

Henry Cuyler Bunner

Henry Cuyler Bunner, for several years the editor of *Punch,*
was born at Oswego, New York, in 1855, and died at Nutley, New
Jersey, in 1896. His poems are noted for their grace and lightness
of touch.

Youth and coquetry predominate in this poem, but there is an
undertone of tragedy which should not be neglected.

I TAKE my chaperon to the play—
  She thinks she is taking me.
And the gilded youth who owns the box,
  A proud young man is he;
But how would his young heart be hurt
  If he could only know
  That not for his sweet sake I go
  Nor yet to see the trifling show;
But to see my chaperon flirt!

Her eyes beneath her snowy hair,
  They sparkle young as mine;
There's scarce a wrinkle in her hand
  So delicate and fine.

And when my chaperon is seen,
　　They come from everywhere—
The dear old boys with silvery hair,
　　With old-time grace and old-time air,
To greet their old-time queen.

They bow as my young Midas here
　　Will never know how to bow
(The dancing masters do not teach
　　That gracious reverence now);
With voices quavering just a bit,
　　They play their old parts through,
　　They talk of folk who used to woo,
　　Of hearts that broke in 'fifty-two—
Now none the worse for it.

And as those aged crickets chirp,
　　I watch my chaperon's face,
And see the dear old features take
　　A new and tender grace;
And in her happy eyes I see
　　Her youth awakening bright,
　　With all its hope, desire, delight—
　　Ah, me! I wish that I were quite
As young—as young as she!

Reprinted by permission of, and by special arrangement with, Charles Scribner's Sons.

America the Beautiful

Katharine Lee Bates

Katharine Lee Bates was born in Falmouth, Mass., in 1859. She is a graduate of the class of 1880 at Wellesley College. Since 1888 she has been professor of English literature in the same institution. She has traveled extensively in Europe and the Orient. Among her numerous publications may be mentioned, "College Beautiful and Other Poems," "English Religious Drama," and "Story of Chaucer's Canterbury Pilgrims, Retold for Children."

Let affection and oratorical fervor characterize the reading of this exquisite poem. It is perhaps best read from the book, after some explanatory introduction to the effect that the author is apostrophizing America.

O BEAUTIFUL for spacious skies,
For amber waves of grain,
For purple mountain majesties
Above the fruited plain!
America! America!
God shed His grace on thee
And crown thy good with brotherhood
From sea to shining sea!

O beautiful for pilgrim feet,
Whose stern, impassioned stress
A thoroughfare for freedom beat
Across the wilderness!
America! America!
God mend thine every flaw,
Confirm thy soul in self-control,
Thy liberty in law!

O beautiful for heroes proved
In liberating strife,

Who more than self their country loved,
  And mercy more than life!
    America!   America!
  May God thy gold refine
Till all success be nobleness
  And every gain divine!

O beautiful for patriot dream
  That sees beyond the years
Thine alabaster cities gleam
  Undimmed by human tears!
    America! · America!
  God shed His grace on thee
And crown thy good with brotherhood
  From sea to shining sea!

Reprinted by permission of the author.

The Caravels of Columbus

Elias Lieberman

Elias Lieberman was born in Petrograd, Russia, in 1883. He was graduated from the College of the City of New York, and is at present Head of the English Department in the Bushwick High School, New York City. He has written plays, short stories, and essays, in addition to his poetry.

In its thought this poem is a happy combination of Joaquin Miller's "Sail On" and Longfellow's "Ship of State." The selection should be delivered with directness and strength.

HE kept them pointed straight ahead—
  Due west they sailed toward shores unknown.
The fearless leader standing deep
  In thought, beside the helm—alone.
He heard about him snarls of rage,

He scanned the frowns of those who plot
Revolt, and day by day he saw
　　But sea and sky, yet faltered not!

And, day by day, he swept in vain
　　Along the dim horizon line.
From castellated sterns his men
　　Gazed down and murmured—angry kine,
Alert to start a wild stampede
　　For home and fodder.　This he bore
With iron will until the day
　　When hope's fruition brought the shore.

His caravels in modern times
　　Can never make the ports that be;
In fancy's fleet they drift along
　　Unchartered wastes from sea to sea,
But he who kept them westward bound
　　So long ago is still alive;
His spirit stirs the trumpet call
　　Wherever men of courage strive.

Our ship of state is sailing, too,
　　On water wild and perilous;
The lightning strikes the troubled mere
　　And shakes the God-like faith of us,
Yet we, like him, must steer the ship
　　Until it leaves the heaving sea
And finds a haven safe and sound
　　Within the port of Loyalty.

Reprinted by permission of the author.

Pioneers

Badger Clark

Badger Clark was born at Albia, Iowa, in 1883. He now lives in The Black Hills of South Dakota. Louis Untermeyer in his "American and British Poetry" says of him: "Clark is one of the few men who have lived to see their work become part of folk-lore, many of his songs having been adapted and paraphrased by the cowboys who have made them their own. There is wind in his songs; the smell of camp-smoke; and the colors of prairie sunsets rise from them." His most famous works are "Sun and Saddle Leather" and "Grass-Grown Trails."

A wide sweep of the imagination and a keen visualization of the westward march of American civilization are required for an adequate vocal interpretation of this fine poem.

A BROKEN wagon wheel that rots away beside the
      river,
   A sunken grave that dimples on the bluff above
         the trail;
The larks call, the wind sweeps, the prairie grasses
         quiver
   And sing a wistful roving song of hoof and wheel
         and sail.
Pioneers, pioneers, you trailed it on to glory,
   Across the circling deserts to the mountains blue
         and dim.
New England was a night camp; Old England was
         a story,
   The new home, the true home, lay out beyond the
         rim.

You fretted at the old hearth, the kettle and the
         cricket,
   The fathers' little acres, the wood lot and the
         pond.

Ay, better storm and famine and the arrow from the
    thicket,
    Along the trail to wider lands that glimmered out
      beyond.
Pioneers, pioneers, the quicksands where you wal-
    lowed,
    The rocky hills and thirsty plains—they hardly
      won your heed.
You snatched the thorny chance, broke the trail that
    others followed
    For sheer joy, for dear joy of marching in the
      lead.

Your wagon track is laid with steel; your tired dust
    is sleeping.
    Your spirit stalks the valleys where a restive na-
      tion teems.
Your soul has never left them in their sowing, in
    their reaping.
    The children of the outward trail, their eyes are
      full of dreams.
Pioneers, pioneers, your children will not reckon
    The dangers on the dusky ways no man has ever
      gone.
They look beyond the sunset where the better coun-
    tries beckon,
    With old faith, with bold faith to find a wider
      dawn.

Reprinted by permission of the author and Charles
Scribner's Sons. Copyright, 1919, by Charles Scribner's
Sons.

Lincoln, the Man of the People

Edwin Markham

For biographical note concerning Edwin Markham, see "The Man With the Hoe," page 103.

This selection is more oratorical than lyric. It should be delivered directly to the audience with sincerity and power. A superb effect can be secured by a proper rendering of the words "lonesome place" in the last line.

WHEN the Norn Mother saw the Whirlwind Hour
Greatening and darkening as it hurried on,
She left the Heaven of Heroes and came down
To make a man to meet the mortal need.
She took the tried clay of the common road—
Clay warm yet with the genial heat of Earth,
Dashed through it all a strain of prophecy;
Tempered the heap with thrill of human tears;
Then mixed a laughter with the serious stuff.
Into the shape she breathed a flame to light
That tender, tragic, ever-changing face;
And laid on him a sense of the Mystic Powers,
Moving—all hushed—behind the mortal veil.
Here was a man to hold against the world,
A man to match the mountains and the sea.

The color of the ground was in him, the red earth;
The smack and tang of elemental things:
The rectitude and patience of the cliff;
The good-will of the rain that loves all leaves;
The friendly welcome of the wayside well;
The courage of the bird that dares the sea;
The gladness of the wind that shakes the corn;

The pity of the snow that hides all scars;
The secrecy of streams that make their way
Under the mountain to the rifted rock;
The tolerance and equity of light
That gives as freely to the shrinking flower
As to the great oak flaring to the wind—
To the grave's low hill as to the Matterhorn
That shoulders out the sky.
Sprung from the West,
He drank the valorous youth of a new world.
The strength of virgin forests braced his mind,
The hush of spacious prairies stilled his soul.
His words were oaks in acorns; and his thoughts
Were roots that firmly gripped the granite truth.

Up from log cabin to the Capitol;
One fire was on his spirit, one resolve—
To send the keen ax to the root of wrong,
Clearing a free way for the feet of God.
And evermore he burned to do his deed
With the fine stroke and gesture of a king:
He built the rail-pile as he built the State,
Pouring his splendid strength through every blow,
The conscience of him testing every stroke,
To make his deed the measure of a man.

So came the Captain with the mighty heart;
And when the judgment thunders split the house,
Wrenching the rafters from their ancient rest,
He held the ridgepole up, and spiked again
The rafters for the Home. He held his place—
Held the long purpose like a growing tree—

'Held on through blame and faltered not at praise.
And when he fell in whirlwind, he went down
As when a lordly cedar, green with boughs,
Goes down with a great shout upon the hills,
And leaves a lonesome place against the sky.

Reprinted by permission of the author.

Theodore Roosevelt

•

Leon Huhner

Leon Huhner is a busy attorney in New York City, yet his patriotic ardor compels him to take time now and then to voice in verse his love for his country and its great men.

In the following poem an eloquent and deserved tribute is paid to an outstanding American. Slow rate and large volume are required to voice effectively this eulogy.

GIGANTIC figure of a mighty age!
How shall I chant the tribute of thy praise,
As statesman, soldier, scientist, or sage?
Thou wert so great in many different ways!
And yet in all there was a single aim—
To fight for truth with sword and tongue and pen!
In wilderness, as in the halls of fame,
Thy courage made thee master over men.
Like some great magnet, that from distant poles
Attracts the particles and holds them fast,
So thou didst draw all men, and fill their souls
With thy ideals,—naught caring for their past,
Their race or creed.   There was one only test:
To love our country and to serve it best!

Reprinted by permission of the author.

The West

Douglas Malloch

Douglas Malloch was born in Muskegon, Mich, May 5, 1877. He began working in Detroit as newspaper reporter, and after some years was made editor. He has written some prose and a great deal of verse relating to the forest and lumber camps, and contributes to the leading magazines.

A world-wide vision is necessary for a correct interpretation of this poem. Note that the *for* in the second line means *because,* and is not the same in meaning as the *for* in the first line. Care will be needed in determining the antecedent of *they* in first line of the second stanza.

MEN look to the East for the dawning things, for
    the light of a rising sun,
But they look to the West, to the crimson West, for
    the things that are done, are done.
The eastward sun is a new-made hope from the dark
    of the night distilled;
But the westward sun is a sunset sun, is the sun of
    a hope fulfilled!

So out of the East they have always come, the
    cradle that saw the birth
Of all the heart-warm hopes of man and all of the
    hopes of earth—
For out of the East arose a Christ and out of the
    East has gleamed
The dearest dream and the clearest dream that ever
    a prophet dreamed.

And into the waiting West they go with the dream-
    child of the East,

And find the hopes that they hoped of old are a
    hundred-fold increased.
For here in the East we dream our dreams of the
    things we hope to do,
And here in the West, the crimson West, the dreams
    of the East come true!

Reprinted by permission of the author.

Out Where the West Begins

Arthur Chapman

Arthur Chapman is a newspaper man residing in New York City.
He was born in Rockford, Illinois, in 1873. He has published
several volumes of verse, becoming famous through the poem
"Out Where the West Begins," originally published in a Denver
newspaper.

This praise of the West of course seems extravagant to those
not living in the West. To read it with the true spirit of the
Westerner, however, it should be given the buoyant fervor of
sincerity.

OUT where the handclasp's a little stronger,
Out where the smile dwells a little longer,
    That's where the West begins;
Out where the sun is a little brighter,
Where the snows that fall are a trifle whiter,
Where the bonds of home are a wee bit tighter,
    That's where the West begins.

Out where the skies are a trifle bluer,
Out where friendship's a little truer,
    That's where the West begins;
Out where a fresher breeze is blowing,
Where there's laughter in every streamlet flowing,

Where there's more of reaping and less of sowing,
  That's where the West begins.

Out where the world is in the making,
Where fewer hearts in despair are aching,
  That's where the West begins;
Where there's more of singing and less of sighing,
Where there's more of giving and less of buying,
And a man makes friends without half trying—
  That's where the West begins.

Reprinted by permission of, and special arrangement with, Houghton Mifflin and Company, from *A Little Book of Western Verse*. Copyrighted by Houghton Mifflin Company.

The Vale of Shadows

Clinton Scollard

Clinton Scollard, author, and professor of English literature in Hamilton College, was born in Clinton, New York, in 1860. He has been a prolific writer of poetry since 1884, having published upward of thirty volumes. In 1915 he published "The Vale of Shadows and Other Poems."

Music in a minor key is found in the following selection. Make much of the rhythm, and tinge the tone with sadness, resignation, and yet with a certain confidence that the evil War Lords must atone for their misdeeds. The pictures can be well developed, but they are always seen through the mist of sadness.

THERE is a vale in the Flemish land,
  A vale once fair to see,
Where under the sweep of the sky's wide arch,
Though winter freeze or summer parch,
The stately poplars march and march,
  Remembering Lombardy.

Here are men of the Saxon eyes,
  Men of the Saxon heart,
Men of the fens and men of the Peak,
Men of the Kentish meadows sleek,
Men of the Cornwall cove and creek,
  Men of the Dove and Dart.

Here are men of the kilted clans
  From the heathery slopes that lie
Where the mists hang gray and the mists hang white,
And the deep lochs brood 'neath the craggy height,
And the curlews scream in the moonless night
  Over the hills of the Skye.

Here are men of the Celtic breed,
  Lads of the smile and tear,
From where the loops of the Shannon flow,
And the crosses gleam in the even-glow,
And the halls of Tara now are low,
  And Donegal cliffs are sheer.

And never a word does one man speak,
  Each in his narrow bed,
For this is the Vale of Long Release,
This is the Vale of the Lasting Peace,
Where wars, and the rumors of wars, shall cease,
  The valley of the dead.

No more are they than the scattered scud,
  No more than broken reeds,
No more than shards or shattered glass,

Than dust blown down the winds that pass,
Than trampled wafts of pampas-grass
  When the wild herd stampedes.

In the dusk of death they laid them down
  With naught of murmuring,
And laughter rings through the House of Mirth
To hear the vaunt of the high of birth,
For what are all the kings of earth
  Before the one great King!

And what shall these proud war-lords say
  At foot of His mighty throne?
For there shall dawn a reckoning day,
Or soon or late, come as it may,
When those who gave the sign to slay
  Shall meet His face alone.

What, think ye, will their penance be
  Who have wrought this monstrous crime?
What shall whiten their blood-red hands
Of the stains of riven and ravished lands?
How shall they answer God's stern commands
  At the last assize of Time?

For though we worship no vengeance-god
  Of madness and of ire,
No Presence grim, with a heart of stone,
Shall they not somehow yet atone?
Shall they not reap as they have sown
  Of fury and of fire?

There is a vale in the Flemish land
  Where the lengthening shadows spread
When day, with crimson sandals shod,
Goes home athwart the mounds of sod
That cry in silence up to God
  From the valley of the dead!

Reprinted by permission of the author.

He Went for a Soldier

Ruth Comfort Mitchell Young

Ruth Comfort Mitchell Young was born in San Francisco, and now lives in Los Gatos, California. She has written numerous poems for the better magazines. Her volume, "The Night Court," is published by The Century Company.

Seldom has the tragedy of youth and war been painted so effectively as in this poem. Notice the transition from the gay to the horrible, and then to the last silence of death. Be sure to make the thought of the last stanza clear—the voice should be strong, but should have a good deal of the explanatory inflection.

HE marched away with a blithe young score of him
  With the first volunteers,
Clear-eyed and clean and sound to the core of him,
  Blushing under the cheers.
They were fine, new flags that swung a-flying there,
Oh, the pretty girls he glimpsed a-crying there,
  Pelting him with pinks and with roses—
  Billy, the Soldier Boy!

Not very clear in the kind young heart of him
  What the fuss was about,
But the flowers and the flags seemed part of him—

The music drowned his doubt.
It's a fine, brave sight they were a-coming there
To the gay, bold tune they kept a-drumming there,
  While the boasting fifes shrilled jauntily—
  Billy, the Soldier Boy!

Soon he is one with the blinding smoke of it—
  Volley and curse and groan:
Then he'has done with the knightly joke of it—
  It's rending flesh and bone.
There are pain-crazed animals a-shrieking there
And a warm blood stench that is a-reeking there;
  He fights like a rat in a corner—
  Billy, the Soldier Boy!

There he lies now, like a ghoulish score of him,
  Left on the field for dead:
The ground all round is smeared with the gore of
      him—
  Even the leaves are red.
The Thing that was Billy lies a-dying there,
Writhing and a-twisting and a-crying there;
  A sickening sun grins down on him—
  Billy, the Soldier Boy!

Still not quite clear in the poor, wrung heart of him
  What the fuss was about,
See where he lies—or a ghastly part of him—
  While life is oozing out:
There are loathsome things he sees a-crawling there;
There are hoarse-voiced crows he hears a-calling
      there,

Eager for the foul feast spread for them—
Billy, the Soldier Boy!

How much longer, O Lord, shall we bear it all?
    How many more red years?
Story it and glory it and share it all,
    In seas of blood and tears?
They are braggart attitudes we've worn so long;
They are tinsel platitudes we've sworn so long—
    We who have turned the Devil's Grindstone,
    Borne with the hell called War!

Reprinted by permission of the author from *The Night Court,* published by The Century Company, New York.

The Laughers

Louis Untermeyer

Louis Untermeyer, author, manufacturing jeweller, lecturer, and associate editor of "The Masses," was born in New York City, in 1885. He has published several volumes of poems since 1910 and has contributed critical reviews to the Chicago *Evening Post,* the New York *Times,* and the *Yale Review.*

The poem that follows has three distinct movements. The first is an out-and-out description of the joy of spring. The second is the utter gloom that the news from the front strikes to the heart of the poet. The third is a masterpiece of irony, almost fiendish in its intensity. In the hands of a skillful reader, this selection can be made most effective.

SPRING!
And her hidden bugles up the street.
Spring—and the sweet
Laughter of winds at the crossing;
Laughter of birds and a fountain tossing

Its hair in abandoned ecstasies.
Laughter of trees.
Laughter of shop-girls that giggle and blush;
Laugh of the tug-boat's impertinent fife.
Laughter followed by a trembling hush—
Laughter of love, scarce whispered aloud.
Then, stilled by no sacredness or strife,
Laughter that leaps from the crowd;
Seizing the world in a rush.
Laughter of life. . . .

Earth takes deep breaths like a man who had feared
    he might smother,
Filling his lungs before bursting into a shout . . .
Windows are opened—curtains flying out;
Over the wash-lines women call to each other.
And, under the calling, there surges, too clearly to
    doubt,
Spring, with the noises
Of shrill, little voices;
Joining in "Tag" and the furious chase
Of "I-spy," "Red Rover" and "Prisoner's Base";
Of the roller-skates' whir at the sidewalk's slope,
Of boys playing marbles and girls skipping rope.
And there, down the avenue, behold,
The first true herald of the Spring—
The hand-organ gasping and wheezily murmuring
Its tunes ten-years old . . .
And the music, trivial and tawdry, has freshness
    and magical swing.
And over and under it,

During and after—
The laughter
Of Spring! . . .

And lifted still
With the common thrill,
With the throbbing air, the tingling vapor,
That rose like strong and mingled wines,
I turned to my paper,
And read these lines:
"Now that the Spring is here,
The war enters its bloodiest phase . . .
The men are impatient. . . .
Bad roads, storms and the rigors of the winter
Have held back the contending armies. . . .
But the recruits have arrived,
And are waiting only the first days of warm
        weather. . . .
There will be terrible fighting along the whole line—
Now that Spring has come."

I put the paper down . . .
Something struck out the sun—something unseen;
Something arose like a dark wave to drown
The golden streets with a sickly green.
Something polluted the blossoming day
With the touch of decay.
The music thinned and died;
People seemed hollow-eyed:
Even the faces of children, where gaiety lingers,

Sagged and drooped like banners about to be
 furled—
And Silence laid its bony fingers
On the lips of the world. . . .
A grisly quiet with the power to choke;
A quiet that only one thing broke;
One thing alone rose up thereafter . . .
Laughter!
Laughter of streams running red.
Laughter of evil things in the night;
Vultures carousing over the dead;
Laughter of ghouls.
Chuckling of idiots, cursed with sight.
Laughter of dark and horrible pools.
Scream of the bullets' rattling mirth,
Sweeping the earth.
Laugh of the cannon's poisonous breath . . .
And over the shouts and the wreckage and
 crumbling
The raucous and rumbling
Laughter of death.
Death that arises to sing,—
Hailing the Spring!

Reprinted by permission of the author and Henry Holt
and Company.

I Have a Rendezvous with Death

Alan Seeger

Alan Seeger was born in New York, June 22, 1888. During his boyhood and youth he traveled extensively in the United States and Mexico. He was in Europe when the war broke out, and like many another young American, promptly enlisted. He was killed in battle July 4, 1917, during the advance on Belloy-en-Sauterre. His collected poems have been published by Charles Scribner's Sons.

The following poem is justly ranked as one of the great poems inspired by the war. The peculiar balance of courage and love of life makes a strong appeal. The poem should be read in a serious tone but should not be made too somber.

I HAVE a rendezvous with Death
At some disputed barricade,
When Spring comes back with rustling shade
And apple blossoms fill the air—
I have a rendezvous with Death
When spring brings back blue days and fair.

It may be he shall take my hand
And lead me into his dark land
And close my eyes and quench my breath—
It may be I shall pass him still.
I have a rendezvous with Death
On some scarred slope of battled hill,
When Spring comes round again this year
And the first meadow flowers appear.

God knows 'twere better to be deep
Pillowed in silk and scented down,
When love throbs out in blissful sleep,
Pulse nigh to pulse, and breath to breath,

Where hushed awakenings are dear—
But I've a rendezvous with Death
At midnight in some flaming town,
When Spring trips north again this year.
And I to my pledged word am true,
I shall not fail my rendezvous.

Reprinted by permission of, and by special arrangement with, Charles Scribner's Sons.

Fleurette

Robert William Service

Robert William Service was born in Preston, England, on Jan. 16, 1874. After attending a public school in Glasgow, he emigrated to Canada, where he went into the banking business. He spent eight years traveling in the Yukon and in the Subarctic. He is now engaged exclusively in literature, and has published a number of poems and ballads, dealing chiefly with life in the Yukon.

This poem is a fine example of conversational verse. It has deep emotion, however, and should be rendered with exquisite feeling. If there can be a little choking up of the throat on "Darn it, I couldn't speak," the effect will strike home. Be careful, however, to do this sincerely, and you may expect tears in your own eyes and the eyes of the audience. Some may prefer to read this selection from the book.

THE Wounded Canadian Speaks:
My leg? It's off at the knee.
Do I miss it? Well, some. You see
I've had it since I was born;
And lately a devilish corn.
(I rather chuckle with glee
To think how I've fooled that corn).

But I'll hobble around all right.
It isn't that, it's my face.

Oh, I know I'm a hideous sight,
Hardly a thing in place.
Sort of gargoyle, you'd say.
Nurse won't give me a glass,
But I see the folks as they pass
Shudder and turn away;
Turn away in distress . . .
Mirror enough, I guess.
I'm gay? You bet I *am* gay,
But I wasn't a while ago.
If you'd seen me even to-day,
The darndedest picture of woe,
With this Caliban mug of mine,
So ravaged and raw and red,
Turned to the wall—in fine
Wishing that I was dead . . .
What has happened since then,
Since I lay with my face to the wall,
The most despairing of men?
Listen! I'll tell you all.

That *poilu* across the way,
With the shrapnel wound on his head,
Has a sister; she came to-day
To sit awhile by his bed.
All morning I heard him fret:
"Oh, when will she come, Fleurette?"

Then sudden, a joyous cry;
The tripping of little feet;
The softest, tenderest sigh;
A voice so fresh and sweet;

Clear as a silver bell,
Fresh as the morning dews:
"C'est toi, c'est toi, Marcel!
Mon frère, comme je suis heureuse!"

So over the blanket's rim
I raised my terrible face,
And I saw—how I envied him!
A girl of such delicate grace;
Sixteen, all laughter and love;
As gay as a linnet, and yet
As tenderly sweet as a dove;
Half woman, half child, Fleurette.
Then I turned to the wall again.
(I was awfully blue, you see)
And I thought with a bitter pain:
"Such visions are not for me."
So there like a log I lay,
All hidden, I thought, from view,
When sudden I heard her say:
"Ah! Who is that *malheureux?*"
Then briefly I heard him tell
(However he came to know)
How I'd smothered a bomb that fell
Into the trench, and so
None of my men were hit,
Though it busted me up a bit.

Well, I didn't quiver an eye,
And he chattered and there she sat;
And I fancied I heard her sigh—
But I wouldn't just swear to that.

And maybe she wasn't so bright,
Though she talked in a merry strain,
And I closed my eyes ever so tight,
Yet I saw her ever so plain;
Her dear little tilted nose,
Her delicate, dimpled chin,
Her mouth like a budding rose,
And the glistening pearls within;
Her eyes like the violet:
Such a rare little queen—Fleurette!

And at last when she rose to go,—
The light was a little dim—
I ventured to peep, and so
I saw her, graceful and slim,
And she kissed him and kissed him, and oh
How I envied and envied him!

So when she was gone I said
In rather a dreary voice
To him of the opposite bed:
"Ah, friend, how you must rejoice!
But me, I'm a thing of dread.
For me nevermore the bliss,
The thrill of a woman's kiss."

Then I stopped, for lo! she was there,
And a great light shone in her eyes.
And me! I could only stare,
I was taken so by surprise,
When gently she bent her head:
"May I kiss you, sergeant?" she said.

Then she kissed my burning lips,
With her mouth like a scented flower,
And I thrilled to the finger-tips,
And I hadn't even the power
To say: "God bless you, dear!"
And I felt such a precious tear
Fall on my withered cheek,
And darn it! I couldn't speak.

And so she went sadly away,
And I know that my eyes were wet.
Ah, not to my dying day
Will I forget, forget!
Can you wonder now I am gay?
God bless her, that little Fleurette!

From *Rhymes of a Red Cross Man* by Robert W. Service, author of *The Spell of the Yukon and Other Verses, Ballads of a Cheechako,* and *Ballads of a Bohemian.* Copyright by Barse and Hopkins, New York.

The Pyres

Hermann Hagedorn

Hermann Hagedorn, Jr., was born in New York City in 1882. He has been associated closely with the literary life of Harvard University since his graduation there in 1907, his commencement poem, "A Troop of the Guard," bringing him into prominent notice. He is the author of several plays.

On account of the many flights of the imagination in this poem, it will be best to read it from the book or manuscript. Keep the pictures clear. Develop the music of the selection, and add the mystery and depth of the infinite in the line, "Stars, make room!"

Pyres in the night, in the night!
And the roaring yellow and red.

ooper, trooper, why so white?"
  We are out to gather our dead.
We have brought dry boughs from the bloody wood
  And the torn hill-side;
We have felled great trunks, wet with blood
  Of brothers that died;
We have piled them high for a flaming bed,
Hemlock and ash and pine for a bed,
A throne in the night, a throne for a bed;
And we go to gather our dead.

"There where the oaks loom, dark and high,
  Over the sombre hill,
  Body on body, cold and still,
Under the stars they lie.
There where the silver river runs,
  Careless and calm as fate,
Mowed, mowed by the terrible guns,
  The stricken brothers wait.
There by the smoldering house, and there
Where the red smoke hangs on the heavy air,
Under the ruins, under the hedge,
Cheek by cheek at the forest-edge;
Back to breast, three men deep,
  Hearing not bugle or drum,
In the desperate trench they died to keep,
Under the starry dome they sleep,
  Murmuring, 'Brothers, come!'

"This way! I heard a call
  Like a stag's when he dies.
Under the willows I saw him fall.

Under the willows he lies.
Give me your hand.   Raise him up.
   Lift his head.   Strike a light.
This morning we shared a crust and a cup.
He wants no supper to-night.
Take his feet.   Here the shells
   Broke all day long,
Moaning and shrieking hell's
   Bacchanalian song!
Last night he helped me bear
   Men to hell's fêting.
To-morrow, maybe, somewhere,
   We, too, shall lie waiting."

Pyres in the night, in the night!
   Weary and sick and dumb,
Under the flickering, faint starlight
   The drooping gleaners come.
Out of the darkness, dim
   Shadowy shadow-bearers,
Dragging into the bale-fire's rim
   Pallid death-farers.

Pyres in the night, in the night!
   In the plain, on the hill.
No volleys for their last rite.
   We need our powder—to kill.
High on their golden bed,
Pile up the dead!

Pyres in the night, in the night!
   Torches, piercing the gloom!

Look! How the sparks take flight!
  Stars, stars, make room!

Smoke, that was bone and blood!
  Hark! The deep roar!
It is the souls telling God
  The glory of WAR!

Reprinted by permission of the author from *The Outlook*.

The Road to Babylon

Margaret Adelaide Wilson

Margaret Adelaide Wilson was born at Portland, Oregon, and educated at Bryn Mawr. She has been writing verse and stories for magazines since 1906.

Strive to make effective the delicate affection voiced in this poem. It is as if some mother thinks of her grown-up son still as a little child.

"How far is it to Babylon?
—Threescore, miles and ten.
Can I get there by candle-light?
Yes, and back again."
And while the nurse hummed the old, old, rhyme,
Tucking him in at evening time,
He dreamed how when he grew a man
And traveled free, as big men can,
He'd slip out through the garden gate
To roads where high adventures wait,
And find the way to Babylon,
Babylon, far Babylon,
All silver-towered in the sun!

He's traveled free, a man with men;
(Bitter the scores of miles and ten!)
And now face down by Babylon's wall
He sleeps, nor any more at all
By morning, noon, or candle-light
Or in the wistful summer night
To his own garden gate he'll come.
—Young feet that fretted so to roam
Have missed the road returning home.

Reprinted by permission of the author and Charles Scribner's Sons. Copyright, 1920, by Charles Scribner's Sons.

He Whom a Dream Hath Possessed

Shaemas O'Sheel

Shaemas O'Sheel was born in New York, in 1886. He was educated at Columbia University. He has published *"The Blossoming Bough"* and *"The Light Feet of Goats."*

This is a direct, stalwart proclamation. It should be delivered with a certain exaltation. It is triumphant, and should be uttered with a sense of infinite confidence, superior to all times, and all things. The tone should be full and strong.

HE whom a dream hath possessed knoweth no more
of doubting,
For mist and the blowing of winds and the mouth-
ing of words he scorns;
Not the sinuous speech of schools he hears, but a
knightly shouting,
And never comes darkness down, yet he greeteth
a million morns.

He whom a dream hath possessed knoweth no more
of roaming;

All roads and the flowing of waves and the speediest
    flight he knows,
But wherever his feet are set, his soul is forever
    homing,
And going he comes, and coming he heareth a call
    and goes.

He whom a dream hath possessed knoweth no more
    of sorrow,
At death and the dropping of leaves and the fading
    of sun he smiles,
For a dream remembers no past and scorns the
    desire of a morrow,
And a dream in a sea of doom sets surely the ulti-
    mate isles.

He whom a dream hath possessed treads the impal-
    pable marches,
From the dust of the day's long road he leaps to a
    laughing star,
And the ruin of worlds that fall he views from
    eternal arches,
And rides God's battlefield in a flashing and golden
    car.

Reprinted by permission of Mitchell Kennerley, New
York.

The Man with The Hoe

(Written after seeing Millet's Famous Painting)

Edwin Markham

Edwin Markham was born at Oregon City, Oregon, April 23, 1852. He early moved to California, where, as a boy, he herded sheep and cattle, later becoming an educator. He is the author of several volumes of poetry and has been a contributor to magazines upon social and economic problems. The following poem attracted wide attention when it was first published in 1899, and has been called "the battle-cry of the next thousand years."

The poem should be read from the page, not recited, and should probably be prefaced by a short narrative, giving the circumstances of its composition. The poet may be imagined as looking at the painting and talking. Earnestness and a deep realization of the meaning of the poem should be sought for. Read the poem slowly and bring out the full meaning of every phrase with keen, strong force.

Bowed by the weight of centuries he leans
Upon his hoe and gazes on the ground,
The emptiness of ages in his face,
And on his back the burden of the world.
Who made him dead to rapture and despair,
A thing that grieves not and that never hopes,
Stolid and stunned, a brother to the ox?
Who loosened and let down this brutal jaw?
Whose was the hand that slanted back this brow?
Whose breath blew out the light within this brain?
Is this the Thing the Lord God made and gave
To have dominion over sea and land;
To trace the stars and search the heavens for power:
To feel the passion of Eternity?
Is this the Dream He dreamed who shaped the suns
And marked their ways upon the ancient deep?
Down all the stretch of Hell to its last gulf

There is no shape more terrible than this—
More tongued with censure of the world's blind
    greed—

More filled with signs and portents for the soul—
More fraught with menace to the universe.
What gulfs between him and the seraphim!
Slave of the wheel of labor, what to him
Are Plato and the swing of Pleiades?
What the long reaches of the peaks of song,
The rift of dawn, the reddening of the rose?
Through this dread shape the suffering ages look;
Time's tragedy is in that aching stoop;
Through this dread shape humanity betrayed,
Plundered, profaned and disinherited,
Cries protest to the Judges of the World,
A protest that is also prophecy.

O masters, lords and rulers in all lands,
Is this the handiwork you give to God,
This monstrous thing distorted and soul-quenched?
How will you ever straighten up this shape;
Touch it again with immortality;
Give back the upward looking and the light;
Rebuild in it the music and the dream;
Make right the immemorial infamies,
Perfidious wrongs, immedicable woes?

O masters, lords and rulers in all lands,
How will the Future reckon with this Man?
How answer his brute question in that hour
When whirlwinds of rebellion shake the world?

How will it be with kingdoms and with kings—
With those who shaped him to the thing he is—
When this dumb Terror shall reply to God,
After the silence of the centuries?

Reprinted by permission of the author.

Silence

Edgar Lee Masters

Edgar Lee Masters was born at Garnet, Kansas, Aug. 23, 1869. He attended the high school at Lewistown, Illinois, later studying law. He is a lawyer and the author of many books of poetry and prose. His most famous production is probably "The Spoon River Anthology."

The poem here reproduced is reflective to the highest degree. It should be read slowly, each thought being fully appreciated. The pitch is low and the tone somewhat "covered."

I HAVE known the silence of the stars and of the sea,
And the silence of the city when it pauses,
And the silence of a man and a maid;
And the silence of the sick
When their eyes roam about the room.
And I ask: For the depths,
Of what use is language?
A beast of the field moans a few times
When death takes its young.
And we are voiceless in the presence of realities—
We cannot speak.

A curious boy asks an old soldier
Sitting in front of the grocery store,
"How did you lose your leg?"
And the old soldier is struck with silence,

Or his mind flies away
Because he cannot concentrate it on Gettysburg.
It comes back jocosely
And he says, "A bear bit it off."
And the boy wonders, while the old soldier
Dumbly, feebly lives over
The flash of the guns, the thunder of the cannon,
The shrieks of the slain,
And himself lying upon the ground,
And the hospital surgeons, the knives,
And the long days in bed.
But if he could describe it all
He would be an artist.
But if he were an artist there would be deeper
    wounds
Which he could not describe.

There is the silence of a great hatred,
And the silence of a great love,
And the silence of an embittered friendship.
There is the silence of a spiritual crisis,
Through which your soul, exquisitely tortured,
Comes with visions not to be uttered,
Into a realm of higher life.
There is the silence of defeat.
There is the silence of those unjustly punished;
And the silence of the dying whose hand
Suddenly grips yours.
There is the silence between father and son,
When the father cannot explain his life,
Even though he be misunderstood for it.

There is the silence that comes between husband
    and wife.
There is the silence of those who have failed;
And the vast silence that covers
Broken nations and vanquished leaders.
There is the silence of Lincoln,
Thinking of the poverty of his youth.
And the silence of Napoleon
After Waterloo.
And the silence of Jeanne d'Arc
Saying amid the flames, "Blessed Jesus"—
Revealing in two words all sorrows, all hope.
And there is the silence of age,
Too full of wisdom for the tongue to utter it
In words intelligible to those who have not lived
The great range of life.

And there is the silence of the dead.
If we who are in life cannot speak
Of profound experiences,
Why do you marvel that the dead
Do not tell you of death?
Their silence shall be interpreted
As we approach them.

Reprinted by permission of, and by special arrangement with, The Macmillan Company. Copyrighted by The Macmillan Company.

The Mystic

Cale Young Rice

For biographical note concerning the author, see "The Chant of the Colorado," page 11.

Here is a poem full of music and rhythm. Make the most of the music that you can, not losing sight of the thought. Deliver the "Just beyond lies God" refrain slowly each time, with an impressive pause, not too long, before it.

THERE is a quest that calls me,
  In nights when I am lone,
The need to ride where the ways divide
  The Known from the Unknown.
I mount what thought is near me
  And soon I reach the place,
The tenuous rim where the Seen grows dim
  And the Sightless hides its face.

  I have ridden the wind,
  I have ridden the sea,
  I have ridden the moon and stars.
  I have set my foot in the stirrup seat
  Of a comet coursing Mars.
  And everywhere
  Thro' the earth and air
  My thought speeds, lightning-shod,
  It comes to a place where checking pace
  It cries, "Beyond lies God!"

It calls me out of the darkness,
  It calls me out of sleep,
"Ride! ride! for you must, to the end of Dust!"

It bids—and on I sweep
To the wide outposts of Being,
   Where there is Gulf alone—
And thro' a Vast that was never passed
   I listen for Life's tone.

      I have ridden the wind,
      I have ridden the night,
      I have ridden the ghosts that flee
      From the vaults of death like a chilling breath
      Over eternity.
      And everywhere
      Is the world laid bare—
      Ether and star and clod—
      Until I wind to its brink and find
      But the cry, "Beyond lies God!"

It calls me and ever calls me!
   And vainly I reply,
"Fools only ride where the ways divide
   What is from the Whence and Why!"
I'm lifted into the saddle
   Of thoughts too strong to tame
And down the deeps and over the steeps
   I find—ever the same.

      I have ridden the wind,
      I have ridden the stars,
      I have ridden the force that flies
      With far intent through the firmament
      And each to each allies.
      And everywhere

That a thought may dare
To gallop, mine has trod—
Only to stand at last on the strand
Where just beyond lies God.

Reprinted by permission of the author and The Century Company, the publishers of the author's works, among which are, "Sea Poems," "Shadowy Thresholds," "Songs to A. H. R.," "Wraiths and Realities," "Earth and New Earth," and "Trails Sunward."

Earth

John Hall Wheelock

John Hall Wheelock is a literary worker of note, and has been long connected with the publishing house of Charles Scribner's Sons, N. Y. He is a contributor to *Harper's, Scribner's, The Century,* and other magazines, and has published many volumes of poetry.

poem, "Earth," taken from the author's book, "Dust and Light, shows great depth and breadth. It should be read slowly, with somewhat of grandeur and majesty. At times the style may approach the scriptural.

GRASSHOPPER, your fairy song
And my poem alike belong
To the deep and silent earth
From which all poetry has birth;
All we say and all we sing
Is but as the murmuring
Of that drowsy heart of hers
When from her deep dream she stirs:
If we sorrow or rejoice,
You and I are but her voice.

Deftly does the dust express
In mind her hidden loveliness,

And from her cool silence stream
The cricket's cry and Dante's dream:
For the earth that breeds the trees
Breeds cities too, and symphonies;
Equally her beauty flows
Into a savior, or a rose—
Toiling up the steep ascent
Towards the complete accomplishment
When all dust shall be, the whole
Universe, one conscious soul.

Yea, the quiet and cool sod
Bears in her breast the dream of God.
If you would know what earth is, scan
The intricate, proud heart of man,
Which is the earth articulate,
And learn how holy and how great,
How limitless and how profound
Is the nature of the ground—
How without terror or demur
We may entrust ourselves to her
When we are wearied out, and lay
Our faces in the common clay.

For she is pity, she is love,
All wisdom she, all thoughts that move
About her everlasting breast
Till she gathers them to rest:
All tenderness of all the ages,
Seraphic secrets of the sages,
Vision and hope of all the seers,
All prayer, all anguish, and all tears

Are but the dust, that from her dream
Awakes, and knows herself supreme—
Looks down in dream, and from above
Smiles at herself in Jesus' love.
Christ's love and Homer's art
Are but the workings of her heart;
Through Leonardo's hand she seeks
Herself, and through Beethoven speaks
In holy thunderings around
The awful message of the ground.

The serene and humble mould
Does in herself all selves enfold—
Kingdoms, destinies, and creeds,
Great dreams and dauntless deeds,
Science that metes the firmament,
The high, inflexible intent
Of one for many sacrificed—
Plato's brain, the heart of Christ;
All love, all legend, and all lore
Are in the dust forevermore.

Even as the growing grass
Up from the soil religions pass,
And the field that bears the rye
Bears parables and prophecy.
Out of the earth the poem grows
Like the lily, or the rose;
And all man is, or yet may be,
Is but herself in agony,
Are but earth when she reveals
All that her secret heart conceals

Down in the dark and silent loam,
Which is ourselves, asleep, at home.

Reprinted by permission of the author from his book, *Dust and Light.* Copyright 1919, by Charles Scribner's Sons.

The House of Life

Madison Cawein

For biographical note concerning the author, see "Deserted," page 39.

The splendid courage and heroism of this poem should be rendered with a strong, firm voice. As every line is heavily charged with meaning, the rate should be slow.

THEY are the wise who look before,
　Nor fear to look behind;
Who in the darkness still ignore
　Pale shadows of the mind.

Who, having lost, though loss be much,
　Still dare to dream and do;
For what was shattered at a touch
　It may be mended, too.

The House of Life has many a door
　That leads to many a room;
And only they who look before
　Shall win from out its gloom.

Who stand and sigh and look behind,
　Regretful of past years,
No room of all those rooms shall find
　That is not filled with fears.

'Tis better not to stop or stay;
　But set all fear aside,
Fling wide the door, whate'er the way,
　And enter at a stride.

Who dares, may win to his desire;
　Or failing, reach the tower,
Whereon Life lights the beacon-fire
　Of one immortal hour.

Reprinted by permission of *The Youth's Companion,*
and by permission of, and special arrangement with, E. P.
Dutton and Company.

The Kings

Louise Imogen Guiney

Louise Imogen Guiney was born in Boston, but later resided
in Oxford, England. She is well known as an editor of literary
works, and published several volumes of her own poetry.

This poem, with its splendid heroism, should be delivered in a
firm, strong tone, revealing an unconquerable soul.

A MAN said unto his Angel:
"My spirits are fallen low,
And I cannot carry this battle:
O brother! where might I go?

"The terrible Kings are on me
With spears that are deadly bright;
Against me so from the cradle
Do fate and my fathers fight."

Then said to the man his Angel:
"Thou wavering, witless soul,

Back to the ranks! What matter
To win or lose the whole,

"As judged by the little judges
Who harken not well nor see?
Not thus, by the outer issue,
The Wise shall interpret thee.

"Thy will is the sovereign measure
Of all events of things.
The puniest heart, defying,
Were stronger than all these Kings.

"Though out of the past they gather,
Mind's Doubt, and Bodily Pain,
And pallid Thirst of the Spirit
That is kin to the other twain,

"And Grief, in a cloud of banners,
And ringleted Vain Desires,
And Vice, with the spoils upon him
Of thee and thy beaten sires,—

"While Kings of eternal evil
Yet darken the hills about,
Thy part is with broken sabre
To rise on the last redoubt;

"To fear not sensible failure,
Not covet the game at all,
But fighting, fighting, fighting,
Die, driven against the wall."

Reprinted by permission of, and by special arrangement with, Houghton Mifflin Company.

To-day

Angela Morgan

Angela Morgan was born in Washington, D. C., and was educated at Columbia University and at Chautauqua, N. Y. She began writing early in her life and in 1915 delivered an original poem entitled, "The Battle Cry of Mothers," to the International Congress of Women at The Hague. She has written some fiction and a number of poems, and contributes to several of the leading magazines.

Deliver this inspiring poem with enthusiasm and high heart.

To be alive in such an age!
With every year a lightning page
Turned in the world's great wonder book
Whereon the leaning nations look.
When men speak strong for brotherhood,
For peace and universal good,
When miracles are everywhere
And every inch of common air
Throbs a tremendous prophecy
Of greater marvels yet to be.
  O thrilling age!
  O willing age!
When steel and stone and rail and rod
Become the avenue of God—
A trump to shout His thunder through,
To crown the work that man may do.

To be alive in such an age!
When man, impatient of his cage,
Thrills to the soul's immortal rage
For conquest—reaches goal on goal,
Travels the earth from pole to pole,

Garners the tempests and the tides
And on a Dream Triumphant rides.
When, hid within a lump of clay,
A light more terrible than day
Proclaims the presence of that Force
Which hurls the planets on their course—
    O age with wings!
    O age that flings
A challenge to the very sky
Where endless realms of conquest lie.
When earth, on tiptoe, strives to hear
The message of a sister sphere,
Yearning to reach the cosmic wires
That flash Infinity's desires.

To be alive in such an age!
That thunders forth its discontent
With futile creed and sacrament,
Yet craves to utter God's intent,
Seeing beneath the world's unrest
Creation's huge, untiring quest,
And through Tradition's broken crust
The flame of Truth's triumphant thrust;
Below the seething thought of man
The push of a stupendous Plan.
    O age of strife!
    O age of life!
When Progress rides her chariot high,
And on the borders of the sky
The signals of the century
Proclaim the things that are to be . . .
The rise of woman to her place,

The coming of a nobler race.
To be alive in such an age—
　To live to it,
　To give to it!
Rise, soul, from thy despairing knees.
What if thy lips have drunk the lees?
Fling forth thy sorrow to the wind—
And link thy hope with humankind . . .
The passion of a larger claim
Will put thy puny grief to shame.
Breathe the world thought, do the world deed,
Think hugely of thy brother's need.
And what thy woe, and what thy weal?
Look to the work the times reveal!
Give thanks with all thy flaming heart—
Crave but to have in it a part.
Give thanks and clasp thy heritage—
To be alive in such an age!

Reprinted by permission of, and special arrangement
with, Dodd, Mead and Company.

Work

Angela Morgan

For biographical note concerning the author, see "Today,"
page 116.
This poem should be read with fervor and tensity, but with a
spirit of delight pervading the whole.

WORK!
Thank God for the might of it,
The ardor, the urge, the delight of it—
Work that springs from the heart's desire,
Setting the brain and the soul on fire—

Oh, what is so good as the heat of it,
And what is so glad as the beat of it,
And what is so kind as the stern command,
Challenging brain and heart and hand?

Work!
Thank God for the pride of it,
For the beautiful, conquering tide of it,
Sweeping the life in its furious flood,
Thrilling the arteries, cleansing the blood,
Mastering stupor and dull despair,
Moving the dreamer to do and dare.
Oh, what is so good as the urge of it,
And what is so glad as the surge of it,
And what is so strong as the summons deep,
Rousing the torpid soul from sleep?

Work!
Thank God for the pace of it,
For the terrible, keen swift race of it;
Fiery steeds in full control,
Nostrils a-quiver to meet the goal.
Work, the Power that drives behind,
Guiding the purposes, taming the mind,
Holding the runaway wishes back,
Reining the will to one steady track,
Speeding the energies faster, faster,
Triumphing over disaster.
Oh, what is so good as the pain of it,
And what is so great as the gain of it?
And what is so kind as the cruel goad,
Forcing us on through the rugged road?

Work!
Thank God for the swing of it,
For the clamoring, hammering ring of it,
Passion of labor daily hurled
On the mighty anvils of the world.
Oh, what is so fierce as the flame of it?
And what is so huge as the aim of it?
Thundering on through dearth and doubt,
Calling the plan of the Maker out.
Work, the Titan; Work, the friend,
Shaping the earth to a glorious end,
Draining the swamps and blasting the hills,
Doing whatever the Spirit wills—
Rending a continent apart, ˋ
To answer the dream of the Master heart.
Thank God for a world where none may shirk—
Thank God for the splendor of work!

Reprinted by permission of, and special arrangement with, Dodd, Mead and Company.

The Weather-Vane

Bliss Carman

For biographical note concerning Bliss Carman, see "The Winter Scene," page 37.

In spite of the slight theme of this poem, it is successful on account of the exquisite imaginative treatment of the little mer-maiden. There is much of the child's fairy tale in the selection, and yet somewhat of deep philosophy. Strive to bring out both.

I saw a painted weather-vane
That stood above the sands—

A little shining mermaiden
   That turned and waved her hands.

She turned and turned, and waved and waved,
   Then faced up toward the hill,
Then faced about and back again,
   Then suddenly stood still.

And every time the wind came up
   Out of the great cool sea,
She'd spin and spin and whirl her arms
   As if in dancing glee.

And when the wind came down the road
   With scent of new-mown hay,
She whirled about and danced again
   In ecstasy of play.

It seemed as if her madcap heart
   Could never quite decide
Whether her heaven was on the hill,
   Or on the drifting tide.

And would she rather be a sprite,
   To guard some singing stream,
To sparkle in the Summer field
   And through the forest gleam?

Or would she be an ocean child,
   A spirit of the deep,
To run upon the billows wild
   And in their cradle sleep?

And still she turned and veered between
   The river and the sea.
And many a time I thought her hands
   Were praying to be free.

And then there came a night of storm,
   Of wind and dark and snow,
And in the morn my shining vane
   Had vanished in the blow.

   Reprinted by permission of the author.

Portrait of a Lady

Sarah Northcliffe Cleghorn

Sarah Northcliffe Cleghorn was born at Norfolk, Virginia, February 4, 1876. Some of her books are, "The Turnpike Lady," 1907; "The Spinster," 1916; "Fellow Captains" (with Dorothy Canfield Fisher), 1916; and "Portraits and Protests," 1917.

Can you picture this lady for yourself? Do you not admire her? Bring this deep admiration into your reading.

HER eyes are sunlit hazel:
   Soft shadows round them play.
Her dark hair, smoothly ordered,
   Is faintly touched with gray.
Full of a gentle brightness
   Her look and language are:—
Kind tongue that never wounded,
   Sweet mirth that leaves no scar.

Her dresses are soft lilac
   And silver-pearly gray.
She wears, on meet occasion,

Modes of a by-gone day,
Yet moves with bright composure
  In fashion's pageant set,
Until her world she teaches
  Its costume to forget.
ı

With score of friends foregathered
  Before a cheerful blaze,
She loves good ranging converse
  Of past and future days.
Her best delight (too seldom)
  From olden friends to hear
How fares the small old city
  She left this many a year.

(There is a still more pleasant,
  A cozier converse still,
When, all the guests departed,
  Close comrades talk their fill.
Beside our smoldering fire
  We muse and wonder late;
Commingling household gossip
  With talk of gods and fate.)

All seeming ways of living,—
  Proportion, comeliness,
Authority and order,—
  Her loyal heart possess.
Then with what happy fingers
  She spreads the linen fair
In that great Church of Bishops
  That is her darling care!

And yet I dare to forecast
  What her new name must be
Writ in the mystic volume
  Beside the crystal sea:—
Instead of "True Believer,"
  The golden quill hath penned,
"Of the poor beasts that perish,
  The brave and noble friend."

Reprinted by permission of the author and Charles Scribner's Sons. Copyright 1919.

The Wild Ride

Louise Imogen Guiney

For biographical note concerning the author, see "The Kings," page 114.

Here is life, summed up in a score of lines. Read the poem with courage and heroism, but do not treat the passing interests of life mentioned in the poem with too great scorn or brutality. Perhaps half the beauty of this selection lies in our longing for the pleasures of life, although we know we must leave them.

I HEAR in my heart, I hear in its ominous pulses,
All day, on the road, the hoofs of invisible horses,
All night, from their stalls, the importunate pawing
    and neighing.

Let cowards and laggards fall back! But alert to
    the saddle,
Weatherworn and abreast, go men of our galloping
    legion,
With a stirrup-cup each to the lily of women that
    loves him.

The trail is through dolor and dread, over crags
and morasses;
There are shapes by the way, there are things that
appall or entice us:
What odds? We are Knights of the Grail, we are
vowed to the riding.

Thought's self is a vanishing wing, and joy is a
cobweb,
And friendship a flower in the dust, and glory a
sunbeam:
Not here is our prize, nor, alas! after these our
pursuing.

A dipping of plumes, a tear, a shake of the bridle,
A passing salute to this world and her pitiful beauty;
We hurry with never a word in the track of our
fathers.

I hear in my heart, I hear in its ominous pulses,
All day, on the road, the hoofs of invisible horses,
All night, from their stalls, the importunate pawing
and neighing.

We spur to a land of no name, outracing the storm-
wind;
We leap to the infinite dark like sparks from the
anvil.
Thou leadest, O God! All's well with Thy troopers
that follow.

At the Crossroads

Richard Hovey

For biographical note concerning the author, see "The Sea Gypsy," page 14.

This poem, like the preceding, has a note of high heroism, but friendship here is made to triumph over Fate. Seek a balance between the note of fatalism and the note of friendship.

You to the left and I to the right,
For the ways of men must sever—
And it well may be for a day and a night,
And it well may be forever.
But whether we meet or whether we part
(For our ways are past our knowing),
A pledge from the heart to its fellow heart
On the ways we all are going!
Here's luck!
For we know not where we are going.

Whether we win or whether we lose
With the hands that life is dealing,
It is not we nor the ways we choose,
But the fall of the cards that's sealing.
There's a fate in love and a fate in fight,
And the best of us all go under—
And whether we're wrong or whether we're right,
We win, sometimes, to our wonder.
Here's luck!
That we may not go under!

With a steady swing and an open brow
We have tramped the ways together,

But we're clasping hands at the crossroads now
In the Fiend's own night for weather;
And whether we bleed or whether we smile
In the leagues that lie before us
The ways of life are many a mile
And the dark of Fate is o'er us.
Here's luck!
And a cheer for the dark before us!

You to the left and I to the right,
For the ways of men must sever,
And it well may be for a day and a night
And it well may be forever!
But whether we live or whether we die
(For the end is past our knowing),
Here's two frank hearts and the open sky,
Be a fair or an ill wind blowing!
HERE'S LUCK!
In the teeth of all winds blowing.

Reprinted by permission of, and by special arrangement
with, Small, Maynard and Company.

Martin

Joyce Kilmer

For biographical note concerning the author, see "Roofs," page 63.

Here is a sharp rebuke for modern materialistic standards.
Lively conversational inflections predominate throughout.

WHEN I am tired of earnest men,
   Intense and keen and sharp and clever,
Pursuing fame with brush or pen

Or counting metal discs forever,
Then from the halls of shadowland
    Beyond the trackless purple sea
Old Martin's ghost comes back to stand
    Beside my desk and talk to me.

Still on his delicate pale face
    A quizzical thin smile is showing,
His cheeks are wrinkled like fine lace,
    His kind blue eyes are gray and glowing.
He wears a brilliant-hued cravat,
    A suit to match his soft gray hair,
A rakish stick, a knowing hat,
    A manner blithe and debonair.

How good, that he who always knew
    That being lovely was a duty,
Should have gold halls to wander through
    And should himself inhabit beauty.
How like his old unselfish way
    To leave those halls of splendid mirth
And comfort those condemned to stay
    Upon the bleak and sombre earth.

Some people ask: What cruel chance
    Made Martin's life so sad a story?
Martin? Why, he exhaled romance
    And wore an overcoat of glory.
A fleck of sunlight in the street,
    A horse, a book, a girl who smiled,—
Such visions made each moment sweet
    For this receptive, ancient child.

Because it was old Martin's lot
　　To be, not make, a decoration,
Shall we then scorn him, having not
　　His genius of appreciation?
Rich joy and love he got and gave;
　　His heart was merry as his dress.
Pile laurel wreaths upon his grave
　　Who did not gain, but was, success.

From *The Poems of Joyce Kilmer,* reprinted by permission of George H. Doran Company, Publishers. Copyright 1918.

The Falconer of God

William Rose Benét

William Rose Benét was born at Fort Hamilton, N. Y., Feb. 2, 1886. He was graduated from the Albany Academy in 1904 and obtained the degree of Ph.B. from Sheffield Scientific School in 1907. He was connected with the *Century* Magazine from that time until he went into the Air Service during the War. In 1919, he became editor of *The Nation's Business,* and contributes poems and humorous verse to many American magazines.

This poem involves a highly imaginative conception of the common human experience that a realized desire rarely brings the satisfaction anticipated. The wording is mystic to a large degree, but abounds in beautiful imagery. Read the selection with a good deal of grandeur and majesty.

I FLUNG my soul to the air like a falcon flying.
I said, "Wait on, wait on, while I ride below!
　　I shall start a heron soon
　　In the marsh beneath the moon—
A strange white heron rising with silver on its wings,
　　Rising and crying
　　Wordless, wondrous things;
The secret of the stars, of the world's heart strings,
　　The answer to their woe.

Then stoop thou upon him, and grip and hold
    him so!"

My wild soul waited on as falcons hover.
I beat the reedy fens as I trampled past.
    I heard the mournful loon
    In the marsh beneath the moon.
And then—with feathery thunder—the bird of my
    desire
    Broke from the cover
    Flashing silver fire.
High up among the stars I saw his pinions spire.
    The pale clouds gazed aghast
As my falcon stoopt upon him, gript and held him
    fast.

My soul dropt through the air—with heavenly
    plunder?—
Gripping the dazzling bird my dreaming knew?
    Nay! but a piteous freight,
    A dark and heavy weight
Despoiled of silver plumage, its voice forever
    stilled,—
    All of the wonder
    Gone that ever filled
Its guise with glory. Oh, bird that I have killed,
    How brilliantly you flew
Across my rapturous vision when first I dreamed of
    you!

Yet I fling my soul on high with new endeavor,
And I ride the world below with a joyful mind.

I shall start a heron soon
In the marsh beneath the moon—
A wondrous silver heron its inner darkness fledges!
　I beat forever
　The fens and the sedges.
The pledge is still the same—for all disastrous
　　　pledges,
　All hopes resigned!
My soul still flies above me for the quarry it shall
　　　find.

Reprinted by permission of the author and The Yale
University Press.

Grieve Not for Beauty

Witter Bynner

For biographical note concerning the author, see "Apollo Trou-
badour," page 147.

Here is a pagan philosophy of a high, transcendent order. As
our physical beauty is not lost, but reproduced in a thousand ways
in Nature, so our souls are not lost, but are reproduced in a
thousand ways in the spiritual world. Throughout there runs the
spirit of triumph over death, but withal a quiet resignation. In
rendering this poem, the voice should be clear, yet speak from out
a hushed silence, as if in the "vasty halls of death."

ALMOST the body leads the laggard soul; bidding it
　　see
The beauty of surrender, the tranquillity
Of fusion with the earth.　The body turns to dust
Not only by a sudden whelming thrust
Or at the end of a corrupting calm,
But oftentimes anticipates, and entering flowers and
　　trees

Upon a hillside or along the brink
Of streams, encounters instances
Of its eventual enterprise:
Inhabits the enclosing clay,
In rhapsody is caught away
In a great tide
Of beauty, to abide
Translated through the night and day
Of time, and by the anointing balm
Of earth to outgrow decay.

Hark in the wind—the word of silent lips!
Look where some subtle throat, that once had
    wakened lust,
Lies clear and lovely now, a silver link
Of change and peace!
Hollows and willows and a river-bed,
Anemones and clouds,
Raindrops and tender distances
Above, beneath,
Inherit and bequeath
Our far-begotten beauty.   We are wed
With many kindred who were seeming dead.
Only the delicate woven shrouds
Are vanished, beauty thrown aside
To honor and uncover
A deeper beauty—as the veil that slips
Breathless away between a lover
And his bride.

So, by the body, may the soul surmise
The beauty of surrender, the tranquillity

Of fusion: when, set free
From semblance of mortality,
Yielding its dust the richer to endue
A common avenue
Of earth for other souls to journey through,
It shall put on in purer guise
The mutual beauty of its destiny.

And who shall fear for his identity,
And who shall cling to the poor privacy
Of incompleteness, when the end explains
That what pride forfeits, beauty gains!
Therefore, O spirit, as a runner strips
Upon a windy afternoon,
Be unencumbered of what troubles you—
Arise with grace
And greatly go, the wind upon your face!

Grieve not for the invisible transported brow
On which like leaves the dark hair grew;
Nor for the lips of laughter that are now
Laughing inaudibly in sun and dew;
Nor for the limbs that, fallen low
And seeming faint and slow,
Shall alter and renew
Their shape and hue
Like birches white before the moon,
Or a young apple-tree
In spring, or the round sea;
And shall pursue
More ways of swiftness than the swallow dips

Among . . . and find more winds than ever blew
The straining sails of unimpeded ships!

For never beauty dies
That lived.   Nightly the skies
Assemble stars, the light of many eyes,
And daily brood on the communal breath—
Which we call death.

Reprinted by permission of, and special arrangement
with, Alfred A. Knopf, Inc.

To the Dead in the Graveyard
Underneath My Window

Adelaide Crapsey

Adelaide Crapsey was born at Rochester, New York, in 1878.
She graduated from Vassar in 1901. She became instructor in
Poetics at Smith College in 1911, but failing health compelled her
to retire in 1913. Between 1913 and 1914, when she died, she
did most of her poetic writing.

What fine rebellion here! How the spirit chafes at the bonds
of the broken body! Lively inflections characterize the whole poem,
with the exception of the last few lines.

How can you lie so still?   All day I watch
And never a blade of all the green sod moves
To show where restlessly you turn and toss,
Or fling a desperate arm or draw up knees
Stiffened and aching from their long disuse.
I watch all night, and not one ghost comes forth
To take its freedom of the midnight hour.
Oh, have you no rebellion in your bones?
The very worms must scorn you where you lie—
A pallid, mouldering, acquiescent folk,
Meek habitants of unresented graves.

Why are you there in your straight row on row,
Where I must ever see you from my bed
That in your mere dumb presence iterate
The text so weary in my ears: "Lie still
And rest—be patient, and lie still and rest."
I'll not be patient! I will not lie still!
There is a brown road runs between the pines,
And further on the purple woodlands lie,
And still beyond blue mountains lift and loom;
And I would walk the road, and I would be
Deep in the wooded shade, and I would reach
The windy mountain-tops that touch the clouds.
My eyes may follow but my feet are held.
Recumbent as you others, must I too
Submit?—be mimic of your movelessness,
With pillow and counterpane for stone and sod?
And if the many sayings of the wise
Teach of submission, I will not submit,
But with a spirit all unreconciled
Flash an unquenched defiance to the stars.
Better it is to walk, to run, to dance;
Better it is to laugh and leap and sing,
To know the open skies of dawn and night,
To move untrammeled down the flaming noon:
And I will clamor it through weary days,
Keeping the edge of deprivation sharp;
Nor with the pliant speaking on my lips
Of resignation, sister to defeat.
I'll not be patient! I will not lie still!

And in ironic quietude who is
The despot of our days and lord of dust

Needs but, scarce heeding, wait to drop
Grim casual comment on rebellion's end;
"Yes, yes. . . . Wilful and petulant, but now
As dead and quiet as the others are."
And this each body and ghost of you hath heard
That in your graves do therefore lie so still.

Reprinted from *Verse* by Adelaide Crapsey, by permission of Alfred A. Knopf, Inc., authorized publishers.

Mother Earth

Harriet Monroe

Harriet Monroe is editor of *Poetry*, and, with Alice Corbin Henderson, is the compiler of "The New Poetry," a collection of modern verse published by The Macmillan Company, New York, in 1917, and in 1923. Her volumes of poetry include "The Passing Show," published by Houghton Mifflin Company, and "You and I," published by The Macmillan Company.

Be sure you grasp the wide sweep of imagination in this poem. Bring out the triumph that is found in Man. Do not neglect, however, the music of the lines.

Oh, a grand old time has the earth
In the long long life she lives!
From her huge mist-shrouded birth,
When, reeling from under,
She tore space asunder,
And, feeling her way
Through the dim first day,
Rose wheeling to run
In the path of the sun—
From then till forever,
Tiring not, pausing never,
She labors and laughs and gives.

Plains and mountains
She slowly makes,
With mighty hand
Sifting the sand,
Lifting the land
Out of the soft wet clutch of the shouting sea.
At lofty fountains
Her thirst she slakes,
And over the hills
Through the dancing rills
Wide rivers she fills,
That shine and sing and leap in their joy to be free.
Cool greenness she needs
And rich odor of bloom;
And longing, believing,
Slowly conceiving,
Her germ-woof weaving,
She spawns little seeds
By the fieldful, the worldful,
And laughs as the pattern grows fair at her loom.

Proudly she trails
Her flower-broidered dresses
In the sight of the sun.
Loudly she hails
Through her far-streaming tresses
His racers that run.
For her heart, ever living, grows eager for life,
Its delight and desire;
She feels the high praise of its passion and strife,
Of its rapture and fire.
There are wings and songs in her trees,

There are gleaming fish in her seas;
The brute beasts brave her
And gnaw her and crave her;
And out of the heart of these
She wrests a dream, a hope,
An arrogant plan
Of life that shall meet her,
Shall know and complete her,
That through ages shall climb and grope,
And at last be Man.

Out of the bitter void she wins him—
Out of the night;
With terror and wild hope begins him,
And fierce delight.
She beats him into caves,
She starves and spurns him.
Her hills and plains are graves—
Into dust she turns him.
She teaches him war and wrath
And waste and lust and greed;
Then over his blood-red path
She scatters her fruitful seed.
With bloom of a thousand flowers,
With songs of the summer hours,
With the love of the wind for the tree,
With the dance of the sun on the sea,
She lulls and quells him—
Oh soft her caress!
And tenderly tells him
Of happiness
Through her ages of years,

Through his toil and his tears.
At her wayward pleasure
She yields of her treasure
A gleam, a hope,
Even a day of days
When the wide heavens ope
And he loves and prays.
Then she laughs in wonder
To see him rise
Her leash from under
And brave the skies!

Oh, a grand old time has the earth
In the long long life she lives!—
A grand old time at her work sublime
As she labors and laughs and gives!

Reprinted by permission of the author from her book,
You and I, published by The Macmillan Company.

Beyond the Stars

Charles Hanson Towne

Charles Hanson Towne was born at Louisville, Kentucky, in
1877. He is an active journalist, having been editor of *The Smart
Set, The Delineator, The Designer,* and *McClure's* Magazine.
Among his published volumes of poetry are "The Quiet Singer,"
"Manhattan," "Youth," "Beyond the Stars and Other Poems,"
all published by Mitchell Kennerley, and "Today and Tomorrow,"
and "Autumn Loiterers," published by Geo. H. Doran and Co.,
New York.

Here is another voice proclaiming the same philosophy as is
found in Witter Bynner's "Grieve not for Beauty." The tone is
strong and rapturous. Give the imagination free rein, and deliver
with fervor.

THREE days I heard them grieve when I lay dead,
(It was so strange to me that they should weep!)

Tall candles burned about me in the dark,
And a great crucifix was on my breast,
And a great silence filled the lonesome room.

I heard one whisper, "Lo! the dawn is breaking,
And he has lost the wonder of the day."
Another came whom I had loved on earth,
And kissed my brow and brushed my dampened
    hair.
Softly she spoke: "Oh, that he should not see
The April that his spirit bathed in! Birds
Are singing in the orchard, and the grass
That soon will cover him is growing green.
The daisies whiten on the emerald hills,
And the immortal magic that he loved
Wakens again—and he has fallen asleep."
Another said: "Last night I saw the moon
Like a tremendous lantern shine in heaven,
And I could only think of him—and sob.
For I remembered evenings wonderful
When he was faint with life's sad loveliness,
And watched the silver ribbons wandering far
Along the shore, and out upon the sea.
Oh, I remembered how he loved the world,
The sighing ocean and the flaming stars,
The everlasting glamour God has given—
His tapestries that wrap the earth's wide room.
I minded me of mornings filled with rain
When he would sit and listen to the sound
As if it were lost music from the spheres.
He loved the crocus and the hawthorn-hedge,
He loved the shining gold of buttercups,

And the low droning of the drowsy bees
That boomed across the meadows. He was glad
At dawn or sundown; glad when Autumn came
With her worn livery and scarlet crown,
And glad when Winter rocked the earth to rest.
Strange that he sleeps today when life is young,
And the wild banners of the Spring are blowing
With green inscriptions of the old delight."

I heard them whisper in the quiet room.
I longed to open then my sealèd eyes,
And tell them of the glory that was mine.
There was no darkness where my spirit flew,
There was no night beyond the teeming world.
Their April was like winter where I roamed;
Their flowers were like stones where now I fared.
Earth's day! it was as if I had not known
What sunlight meant! . . . Yea, even as they
    grieved
For all that I had lost in their pale place,
I swung beyond the borders of the sky,
And floated through the clouds, myself the air,
Myself the ether, yet a matchless being
Whom God had snatched from penury and pain
To draw across the barricades of heaven.
I climbed beyond the sun, beyond the moon;
In flight on flight I touched the highest star;
I plunged to regions where the spring is born,
Myself (I asked not how) the April wind,
Myself the elements that are of God.
Up flowery stairways of eternity
I whirled in wonder and untrammeled joy,

An atom, yet a portion of His dream—
His dream that knows no end. . . .

                           I was the rain,
I was the dawn, I was the purple east,
I was the moonlight on enchanted nights,
(Yet time was lost to me) ; I was a flower
For one to pluck who loved me; I was bliss,
And rapture, splendid moments of delight;
And I was prayer, and solitude, and hope;
And always, always, always I was love.
I tore asunder flimsy doors of time,
And through the windows of my soul's new sight
I saw beyond the ultimate bounds of space.
I was all things that I had loved on earth—
The very moonbeam in that quiet room,
The very sunlight one had dreamed I lost,
The soul of the returning April grass,
The spirit of the evening and the dawn,
The perfume in unnumbered hawthorn-blooms.
There was no shadow on my perfect peace,
No knowledge that was hidden from my heart.
I learned what music meant; I read the years;
I found where rainbows hide, where tears begin;
I trod the precincts of things yet unborn.

Yea, while I found all wisdom (being dead)
They grieved for me. . . . I should have grieved
    for them!

Reprinted by permission of Mitchell Kennerley, New York.

The Unconquered Air

Florence Earle Coates

Florence Earle Coates was born in Philadelphia, and educated at private schools in that city and in France and Belgium. She has published several volumes of poems, which were collected in two volumes and published in 1916.

Pride, majesty, and superiority mark the early part of this poem. In the second part admiration for man's heroism is the predominant note. The whole poem is upon an exalted plane, and should not be made trivial in any part.

1

OTHERS endure Man's rule: he therefore deems
  I shall endure it—I, the unconquered Air!
  Imagines this triumphant strength may bear
His paltry sway! yea, ignorantly dreams,
Because proud Rhea now his vassal seems,
  And Neptune him obeys in billowy lair,
  That he a more sublime assault may dare,
Where blown by tempest wild the vulture screams!

Presumptuous, he mounts: I toss his bones
  Back from the height supernal he has braved:
Ay, as his vessel nears my perilous zones,
I blow the cockle-shell away like chaff
  And give him to the Sea he has enslaved.
He founders in its depths; and then I laugh!

2

Impregnable I held myself, secure
  Against intrusion.   Who can measure Man?
  How should I guess his mortal will outran

Defeat so far that danger could allure
For its own sake?—that he would all endure,
   All sacrifice, all suffer, rather than
    Forego the daring dreams Olympian
That prophesy to him of victory sure?

Ah, tameless courage!—dominating power
That, all attempting, in a deathless hour
   Made earth-born Titans godlike, in revolt!—
Fear is the fire that melts Icarian wings:
Who fears nor Fate, nor Time, nor what Time
    brings,
   May drive Apollo's steeds, or wield the thunder-
    bolt!

Reprinted by permission of, and by special arrangement with, Houghton Mifflin Company, Boston, the authorized publishers.

I Shall Not Pass This Way Again

Eva Rose York

Mrs. Eva Rose York was born in Western Ontario in 1858. She was educated at Woodstock College and at the New England Conservatory of Music. She has written much occasional verse. At present her residence is Toronto, Canada.

This poem is truly "A Symphony." The music of the verse is surpassingly rare. Make much of the prayer for forgiveness. Throughout the spirit of beauty is tinged with sadness.

I SHALL not pass this way again—
   Although it bordered be with flowers,
   Although I rest in fragrant bowers,
     And hear the singing
     Of song-birds winging

To highest heaven their gladsome flight;
Though moons are full and stars are bright,
And winds and waves are softly sighing,
While leafy trees make low replying;
Though voices clear in joyous strain
Repeat a jubilant refrain;
Though rising suns their radiance throw
On summer's green and winter's snow
In such rare splendor that my heart
Would ache from scenes like these to part;
  Though beauties heighten,
  And life-lights brighten,
And joys proceed from every pain,—
I shall not pass this way again.

Then let me pluck the flowers that blow,
And let me listen as I go
  To music rare
  That fills the air;
  And let hereafter
  Songs and laughter
Fill every pause along the way;
And to my spirit let me say:
"O soul, be happy; soon 'tis trod,
The path made thus for thee by God.
Be happy, thou, and bless His name
By whom such marvelous beauty came."
And let no chance by me be lost
To kindness show at any cost.
I shall not pass this way again;
Then let me now relieve some pain,
Remove some barrier from the road,

Or brighten someone's heavy load;
A helping hand to this one lend,
Then turn some other to befriend.

    O God, forgive
    That now I live
As if I might, sometime, return
To bless the weary ones that yearn
For help and comfort every day,—
For there be such along the way.
O God, forgive that I have seen
The beauty only, have not been
Awake to sorrow such as this;
That I have drunk the cup of bliss
Remembering not that those there be
Who drink the dregs of misery.

I love the beauty of the scene,
Would roam again o'er fields so green;
But since I may not, let me spend
My strength for others to the end,—
For those who tread on rock and stone,
And bear their burdens all alone,
Who loiter not in leafy bowers,
Nor hear the birds nor pluck the flowers.
A larger kindness give to me,
A deeper love and sympathy;
    Then, Oh, one day
    May someone say—
Remembering a lessened pain—
"Would she could pass this way again!"

Taken by permission from *"A Treasury of Canadian Verse,"* published by E. P. Dutton and Company.

Apollo Troubadour

Witter Bynner

Witter Bynner was born at Brooklyn, N. Y., August 10, 1881. He is a graduate of Harvard and has been editor of several leading magazines. He was instructor in English at the University of California in 1918-1919. He has written a number of plays and poems, and contributes to various magazines.

Can you hear the hand-organ through this melody of words? Bring out the music, but let the wildly fantastic pictures steal gently through it all—almost as if the pictures were seen half dimly through a silken veil.

WHEN a wandering Italian
Yesterday at noon
Played upon his hurdy-gurdy
Suddenly a tune,
There was magic in my ear-drums:
Like a baby's cup and spoon
Tinkling time for many sleigh-bells,
Many no-school, rainy-day-bells,
Cow-bells, frog-bells, run-away-bells,
Mingling with an ocean medley
As of elemental people
More emotional than wordy—
Mermaids laughing off their tantrums,
Mermen singing loud and sturdy,—
Silver scales and fluting shells,
Popping weeds and gurgles deadly,
Coral chime from coral steeple,
Intermittent deep-sea bells,
Ringing over floating knuckles,
Buried gold and swords and buckles,
And a thousand bubbling chuckles,

Yesterday at noon—
Such a melody as starfish,
And all fish that really are fish.
In a gay remote battalion
Play at midnight to the moon!

Could any playmate on our planet,
Hid in a house of earth's own granite,
Be so devoid of primal fire
That a wind from this wild crated lyre
Should find no spark and fan it?
Would any lady half in tears,
Whose fashion, on a recent day
Over the sea, had been to pay
Vociferous gondoliers,
Beg that the din be sent away
And ask a gentleman, gravely treading
As down the aisle at his own wedding
To toss the foreigner a quarter
Bribing him to leave the street;
That motor-horns and servants' feet
Familiar might resume, and sweet
To her offended ears,
The money-music of her peers!

Apollo listened, took the quarter
With his hat off to the buyer,
Shrugged his shoulder small and sturdy,
Led away his hurdy-gurdy
Street by street, then turned at last
Toward a likelier piece of earth

Where a stream of chatter passed,
Yesterday at noon;
By a school he stopped and played
Suddenly a tune. . . .
What a melody he made!
Made in all those eager faces,
Feet and hands and fingers!
How they gathered, how they stayed
With smiles and quick grimaces,
Little man and little maid!
How they took their places,
Hopping, skipping, unafraid,
Darting, rioting about,
Squealing, laughing, shouting out!
How, beyond a single doubt,
In my own feet sprang the ardor
(Even now the motion lingers)
To be joining in their paces!
Round and round the handle went,—
Round their hearts went harder;—
Apollo urged the happy rout
And beamed, ten times as well content
With every son and daughter
As though their little hands had lent
The gentleman his quarter.
(You would not guess—nor I deny—
That that same gentleman was I!)

No gentleman may watch a god
With proper happiness therefrom;
So street by street again I trod

The way that we had come.
He had not seen me following
And yet I think he knew;
For still, the less I heard of it
The more his music grew;
As if he made a bird of it
To sing the distance through . . .
And, O Apollo, how I thrilled,
You liquid-eyed rapscallion,
With every twig and twist of spring,
Because your music rose and filled
Each leafy vein with dew—
With melody of olden sleigh-bells,
Over-the-sea-and-far-away-bells,
And the heart of an Italian,
And the tinkling cup and spoon,—
Such a melody as star-fish,
And all fish that really are fish,
In a gay remote battalion
Play at midnight to the moon!

Reprinted by permission of the author and by permission of, and by special arrangement with, Alfred A. Knopf, Inc., New York, the publisher of the author's works.

In Blossom Time

Ina Donna Coolbrith

Ina Donna Coolbrith was born in Illinois, but came to California in her early childhood. She is a member of a number of societies and clubs in the West and is the only woman member of the Bohemian Club in San Francisco. She was invested with the poet laureateship of California in 1915. She is the author of a large number of poems, and contributes to the leading magazines of the country.

This poem is almost pure music—the music of delight and freedom. Come as close to singing as you can and yet talk. Develop as beautiful and fitting a melody as you can.

It's O my heart, my heart,
    To be out in the sun and sing,
To sing and shout in the fields about,
    In the balm and blossoming.

Sing loud, O bird in the tree;
    O bird, sing loud in the sky,
And honey-bees, blacken the clover-bed;
    There are none of you glad as I.

The leaves laugh low in the wind,
    Laugh low with the wind at play;
And the odorous call of the flowers all
    Entices my soul away.

For oh, but the world is fair, is fair,
    And oh, but the world is sweet;
I will out in the gold of the blossoming mould,
    And sit at the Master's feet.

And the love my heart would speak,
    I will fold in the lily's rim,

That the lips of the blossom more pure and meek,
　　May offer it up to Him.

Then sing in the hedgerow green, O thrush,
　　O skylark, sing in the blue;
Sing loud, sing clear, that the King may hear,
　　And my soul shall sing with you.

Reprinted by permission of the author from her book,
Songs of the Golden Gate, published by Houghton Mifflin
Company, Boston.

Tipperary in the Spring

Denis Aloysius McCarthy

Denis Aloysius McCarthy was born in Ireland, July 25, 1870.
He later came to United States and became an editorial writer
for *The Herald,* Boston, and other publications. He devotes him-
self to editorials and to lecturing on literary, patriotic, and social
topics.

As in so much lyric poetry, the problem here is to maintain the
proper balance between the music and the sense. The lines where
there are syllables lacking to make up the verse should be studied
carefully, in order that they may be made to fit in with the rhythm
of the other, more regular lines.

Ah, sweet is Tipperary in the springtime of the year,
When the hawthorn's whiter than the snow,
When the feathered folk assemble, and the air is all
　　a-tremble
With their singing and their winging to and fro:
When queenly Slievenamon puts her verdant ves-
　　ture on,
And smiles to hear the news the breezes bring,

And the sun begins to glance on the rivulets that
     dance—
Ah, sweet is Tipperary in the Spring!

Ah, sweet is Tipperary in the springtime of the year,
When mists are rising from the lea,
When the Golden Vale is smiling with a beauty all
     beguiling,
And the Suir goes crooning to the sea;
And the shadows and the showers only multiply the
     flowers
That the lavish hand of May will fling;
Where in unfrequented ways, fairy music softly
     plays—
Ah, sweet is Tipperary in the Spring!

Ah, sweet is Tipperary in the springtime of the year,
When life like the year is young,
When the soul is just awaking like a lily blossom
     breaking,
And love words linger on the tongue;
When the blue of Irish skies is the hue of Irish eyes,
And love dreams cluster and cling
Round the heart and round the brain, half of pleas-
     ure, half of pain—
Ah, sweet is Tipperary in the Spring!

Reprinted by permission. Copyrighted by Little, Brown and Company.

The Drum

Edward Forrester Sutton

Edward Forrester Sutton lives at 248 Central Park West, New York City. He has written much verse for current magazines. As yet his poems have not been published in book form, but a collection is being contemplated.

This is a selection that would delight the old-time elocutionist. Do not carry the imitation of the drum too far. Bring out the import of the poem as you go along. Cast the message of each sort of drum in a different key. Do not forget to slow down the rate of utterance when the muffled drum is reached. Use all the elocution you possess, but use it sensibly, not grotesquely.

THERE'S a rhythm down the road where the elms
      overarch
  Of the drum, of the drum,
There's a glint through the green, there's a column
      on the march,
  Here they come, here they come,
To the flat resounding clank they are tramping rank
      on rank,
And the bayonet flashes ripple from the flank to
      the flank.
    "I am rhythm, marching rhythm," says the
      drum.
"No aid am I desiring of the loud brazen choiring
"Of bugle or of trumpet, the lilt and the lyring,
"I'm the slow dogged rhythm, unending, untiring,
    "I am rhythm, marching rhythm," says the
      drum.
    "I am rhythm, dogged rhythm, and the plod-
      ders feel me with 'em

"I'm the two miles an hour that is empire, that
is power,
"I'm the slow resistless crawl in the dust-cloud's
choking pall,
"I'm the marching days that run from the dawn
to set of sun,
"I'm the rifle and the kit and the dragging
weight of it,
"I'm the jaws grimly set and the faces dripping
sweat,
"I'm the how, why, and when, the Almighty
made for men,"
Says the rhythm, marching rhythm, of the
drum.
"Did you call my song 'barbaric?' Did you mutter,
'out of date'?
"When you hear me with the foemen then your cry
will come too late.
"Here are hearts a-beating for you, to my pulsing
as I come,
"To the rhythm, tramping rhythm,
"To the rhythm, dogged rhythm,
"To the dogged tramping rhythm
"Of the drum!"

There's a clashing snarling rhythm down the valley
broad and ample
Of the drum, kettledrum,
There's a low, swelling rumor that is cavalry
a-trample,
Here they come, here they come,

To the brassy crash and wrangle, to the horseman's
    clink and jangle,
And the restive legs beneath 'em all a-welter and
    a-tangle.
    "I am rhythm, dancing rhythm," says the drum.
"White and sorrel, roan and dapple, hocks as shiny
    as an apple,
"Don't they make a splendid showing, ears a-prick-
    ing, tails a-blowing?
"Good boys—bless 'em—well they're knowing all
    my tricks to set 'em going
        "To my rhythm, clashing rhythm!" says the
        drum.
        "I am rhythm, clashing rhythm, and the horses
        feel me with 'em.
        "I'm the foray and the raid, I'm the glancing
        sabre blade.
        "Now I'm here, now I'm there, flashing on the
        unaware,
        "How I scout before the ranks, how I cloud
        along the flanks,
        "How the highway smokes behind me let the
        faint stars tell that find me
        "All night through, all night through, when the
        bridles drip with dew.
        "I'm the labor, toil, and pain, I'm the loss that
        shall be gain,"
    Says the rhythm, clashing rhythm, of the drum.
"Did you speak of 'useless slaughter'? Did you
    murmur 'Christian love'?
"Pray that such as these before you, when the war-
    cloud bursts above,

"With the bridle on the pommel meet the foemen
　　　　as they come,
　　"To the rhythm, dashing rhythm,
　　"To the rhythm, crashing rhythm
　　"To the crashing, dashing rhythm
　　　　　　"Of the drum!"

There's an echo shakes the valley o'er the rhythm
　　　　deep and slow
　　Of the drum, of the drum,
'Tis the guns, the guns a-rolling on the bridges down
　　　　below,
　　Here they come, here they come,
Hark the felloes grind and lumber through the
　　　　shadows gray and umber,
And the triple spans a-panting up the slope the
　　　　stones encumber,
　　　With the rhythm, distant rhythm, of the
　　　　drum.
" 'Tis the long Shapes of Fear that the moonlight
　　　　silvers here,
"And the jolting limber's weighted with the silent
　　　　cannoneer,
" 'Tis the Pipes of Peace are passing, O ye people,
　　　　give an ear!"
　　　Says the rhythm, iron rhythm, of the drum.
　　"They are rhythm, thunder rhythm, and they
　　　　do not need me with 'em,
　　"That can overtone my choir like the bourdon
　　　　from the spire.
"Avant-garde am I to these Lords of Dreadful
　　　　Revelries,

"Iron Cyclops with an eye to confound the
earth and sky.

"Love and Fear, Love and Fear, neither one but
both revere,

"And whatever grace ye deal let it be from
courts of steel,

"Set the guns' emplacement then to expound
the Law to men,"

Says the rhythm, iron rhythm of the drum.

"O ye coiners, sentence-joiners, in a fatted, trades-
man's land,

"Here's evangel Pentecostal that all nations under-
stand.

"When they speak before the battle fools and
theories are dumb!"

God be with 'em, and the rhythm,

And the rhythm, iron rhythm,

And the rolling thunder rhythm

Of the drum!

There's a rhythm still and toneless with the wind
amid the green,

Of the drum, muffled drum,

And there's arms reversed, and something, 'neath a
flag that goes between

As they come, as they come.

"Just a soldier, nothing more, such as all the ages
bore

"And as time and tide shall bear them till the sun
be sere and hoar,"

Says the rhythm, muffled rhythm, of the drum.

"No more am I requiring of the keen brazen lyring

"Then 'taps' from the bugle—some shots for the
firing.
"Hats off; stand aside; it is all I'm desiring,"
Says the rhythm, muffled rhythm, of the drum.
"I am rhythm, muffled rhythm; long and deep
farewell go with him,
"Hands that bore their portion through tasks
our nature needs must do,
"Feet that stepped the ancient rhyme of the
battle-march of Time.
"Blood or tribute, steel or gold, still *Vae Victis*
as of old,
"Stern and curt the message runs taught to sons
and sons of sons.
"*Chair à canon,* would you call? What else
are we, one and all?
"Write it thus to close his span: 'Here there
lies a fighting man,' "
Says the rhythm, muffled rhythm, of the drum.
"O ye farms upon the hillside, and ye cities by the
sea,
"With the laughter of young mothers and their
babes about the knee,
" 'Tis a heart that once beat for you that is passing,
still and dumb,
"To the rhythm, muffled rhythm,
"To the rhythm, solemn rhythm,
"To the slow and muffled rhythm
"Of the drum!"

Reprinted by permission of the author from *Poems of
the Great War,* published by the Yale University Press.

A Song of Sherwood

Alfred Noyes

Alfred Noyes was born at Staffordshire, England, in 1880, and was educated at Oxford. He has published several volumes of poetry, his works being collected in 1913, and published by Frederick A. Stokes Company, New York. Noyes is noted for his musical rhythms.

Sherwood Forest, in Nottinghamshire, England, formerly of large extent, was the principal scene of the legendary exploits of Robin Hood. If you visualize the scene by reviewing the stories of Robin Hood, no difficulty will be found in reading this beautiful poem.

SHERWOOD in the twilight! Is Robin Hood awake?
Gray and ghostly shadows are gliding through the
    brake,
Shadows of the dappled deer, dreaming of the morn,
Dreaming of a shadowy man that winds a shadowy
    horn.

Robin Hood is here again: all his merry thieves
Hear a ghostly bugle-note shivering through the
    leaves,
Calling as he used to call, faint and far away,
In Sherwood, in Sherwood, about the break of day.

Merry, merry England has kissed the lips of June:
All the wings of fairyland were here beneath the
    moon,
Like a flight of rose-leaves fluttering in a mist
Of opal and ruby and pearl and amethyst.

Merry, merry England is waking as of old,
With eyes of blither hazel and hair of brighter gold:

For Robin Hood is here again beneath the bursting
    spray
In Sherwood, in Sherwood, about the break of day.

Love is in the greenwood building him a house
Of wild rose and hawthorn and honeysuckle boughs:
Love is in the greenwood, dawn is in the skies,
And Marian is waiting with a glory in her eyes.

Hark! The dazzled laverock climbs the golden
    steep!
Marian is waiting: is Robin Hood asleep?
Round the fairy grass-rings frolic elf and fay,
In Sherwood, in Sherwood, about the break of day.

Oberon, Oberon, rake away the gold,
Rake away the red leaves, roll away the mould,
Rake away the gold leaves, roll away the red,
And wake Will Scarlett from his leafy forest
    bed.

Friar Tuck and Little John are riding down together
With quarter-staff and drinking-can and gray goose-
    feather.
The dead are coming back again, the years are rolled
    away
In Sherwood, in Sherwood, about the break of day.

Softly over Sherwood the south wind blows.
All the heart of England hid in every rose
Hears across the greenwood the sunny whisper leap,
Sherwood in the red dawn, is Robin Hood asleep?

Hark, the voice of England wakes him as of old
And, shattering the silence with a cry of brighter
gold,
Bugles in the greenwood echo from the steep,
Sherwood in the red dawn, is Robin Hood asleep?

Where the deer are gliding down the shadowy glen
All across the glades of fern he calls his merry
men—
Doublets of the Lincoln green glancing through the
May
In Sherwood, in Sherwood, about the break of day—

Calls them and they answer: from aisles of oak and
ash
Rings the *Follow!   Follow!* and the boughs begin to
crash,
The ferns begin to flutter and the flowers begin to
fly,
And through the crimson dawning the robber band
goes by.

Robin!   Robin!   Robin! All his merry thieves
Answer as the bugle-note shivers through the leaves,
Calling as he used to call, faint and far away,
In Sherwood, in Sherwood, about the break of day.

Reprinted by permission from *Collected Poems,* by
Alfred Noyes. Copyright 1913 by Frederick A. Stokes
Company.

The Heroes of the Yukon

John Augustus Gilkey

John Augustus Gilkey was born in Troy, Maine, in 1853. He is a lineal descendant of Thomas Rogers of the *Mayflower*, also of Col. Edmund Phinney, an officer of the American Army in the Revolution. He was educated in the public schools of Maine and the University of Washington. The following poem written by him, won first prize in an Oratorical Contest recently held in the State of Oregon.

During the winter of 1924–25, a diphtheria epidemic broke out in Alaska. To add to the horror of the dread disease, there was no more diphtheria serum left in Nome. Word was sent out from the stricken territory asking that diphtheria serum be rushed to the helpless victims. Because of the snow and ice, the serum could not be sent by ordinary means. "Wild Bill" Shannon, the hero of many a Northland tale, offered to rush the precious serum overland with his dog team. The eyes of the world were focused upon his heroic rescue.

Emphasis should be placed on the necessity for quick action to save the "children of Nome who are dying." The poem should therefore be recited in sharp, staccato tones. Be careful, however, to enunciate clearly. The final stanza should be spoken more slowly but exultantly, as if giving a toast to the heroes.

WORD is flashed from the Arctic Sea
       ("Hurry")
That a scourge is stalking in fiendish glee
On snow-clad tundra and frozen lea;
"O! ride as though you were flying!
For a healing balm we sorely need;
Come to our rescue like fiery steed
As he dashes to battle with lightning speed—
For the children of Nome are dying."

To Nenana dog teams are quickly brought;
       ("Hurry")
The dogs are harnessed as quick as thought.
To be a leader each is taught,
And to run as though he were flying

O'er frozen tundra and trackless snow,
For countless leagues the cure must go,
With the temperature sixty degrees below;
For the children of Nome are dying.

"Wild Bill" Shannon grasps the rein;
       ("Hurry")
Each noble dog in that harnessed train
Tugs at his leash with might and main,
To speed as though he were flying
O'er countless miles in storm and sleet,
With scanty rations of reindeer meat,
With frozen ears and bleeding feet—
For the children of Nome are dying.

At Tolovana Jim Kelland's team
       Is ready.
No northern light with its fitful gleam
Will light the pass or the frozen stream
For the faithful dogs that are flying
Through the arctic day and the arctic night,
Unheeding the frost-king's stinging bite,
Unerring as the eagle's flight,
Toward Nome where the children are dying.

Bill Green with his team for the third relay
       Will hurry
To Kallens and Folger who'll speed away
Till Nicholas meets them on the way,
And off through the blizzard flying

Will meet Sepalla the musher king,
Who flies with his famous dogs to bring
The balm of healing—that priceless thing—
To the children of Nome who are dying.

The storm grows fiercer; the wind is wild,
      As they hurry.
As the musher sees the snow-drifts piled,
He thinks of some suffering, stricken child,
And urges his dogs into flying.
His hands are frozen and cracked to the bone,
His dogs call to him with pitiful moan,
But God is watching above his own,
As they speed toward the ones who are dying.

Olson and Rohn, brave knights of the trail,
      How they hurry!
Gunnar Kasson must face an arctic gale
On Norton Sound, he must not fail;
And Balto, his leader, goes flying.
In blinding blizzard and arctic night
He fights his battle, he wins his fight;
In the first gray dawn of the morning light,
He's in Nome, with help for the dying.

    *   *   *   *   *

Bards have sung of the faithful steed
      Which hurries
To bear his master o'er mountain and mead
To battle, or some heroic deed,
And runs as though he were flying;

But here's to the dogs of the Yukon wild,
Which through the passes swiftly filed,
To give their lives for a little child—
For some of those brave dogs are dying.

Let others sing of Sheridan's ride,
Of Paul Revere o'er the country side,
Or Denmark's king to save his bride,
Who rode as though they were flying.
But I'll sing of the mushers true and bold
Who braved the wrath of the arctic cold,
With never a thought of fame or gold,
To save the ones who were dying.